Washington's Prayer for the Nation

Almighty God, we make our earnest prayer that Thou wilt keep the United States in thy holy protection, that Thou wilt incline the hearts of the citizens to cultivate a spirit of subordination and obedience to government, and entertain a brotherly affection and love for one another and for their fellow citizens of the United States at large.

And finally that Thou wilt most graciously be pleased to dispose us all to do justice, to love mercy, and to demean ourselves with that charity, humility, and pacific temper of mind which were the characteristics of the Divine Author of our blessed religion, and without an humble imitation of whose example in these things, we can never hope to be a happy nation.

Grant our supplications, we beseech Thee, through Jesus Christ our Lord. Amen. *(Written at Newburg, June 8, 1783, and sent to the Governors of all the States.)*

Song and Service Book
for
Ship and Field

Army and Navy

Edited by

Ivan L. Bennett
Chairman of the Editorial Committee

UNITED STATES
GOVERNMENT PRINTING OFFICE
WASHINGTON
1942

COPYRIGHT, 1941, BY

A. S. BARNES AND COMPANY, INCORPORATED

*The property rights of the publisher's copyright
in this compilation shall be available to the
Government at all times and without cost.*

PRINTED IN THE UNITED STATES OF AMERICA

Preface

THE NATIONAL CONVENTION of the Chaplains of the Army and Navy in New York City, May, 1940, voted approval of the suggestion of the committee on hymnal that effort be made to replace the word edition of the Army and Navy Hymnal with a service book containing selected hymns with musical score. Grateful acknowledgment is made of the cooperative efforts of the chaplains, publishers, and agencies serving the spiritual needs of our men on land and sea. The compilation has been made during a great national emergency, and the time element has necessitated haste. The prayers and other aids to worship have been selected, not to take the place of prayer book or missal in the ministry of the chaplain, but to furnish aids for congregational participation in public worship. It is our hope that every chaplain will find sufficient data to enrich and extend congregational assistance at the services in field and aboard ship. The orders of service are intended not only as a ready aid to the younger chaplains, but also as a guide to the faithful helpers who carry on divine worship in the absence of a chaplain. To the men, living and dead, who have hazarded their lives for America, to the lads who keep faithful watch today and tomorrow, and to the Glory of Almighty God, we dedicate this Song and Service Book.

ROBERT D. WORKMAN,
Head of the Chaplains' Division,
Bureau of Navigation,
Navy Department.

WILLIAM R. ARNOLD,
Chief of Chaplains,
War Department.

IVAN L. BENNETT, Chaplain, U. S. Army,
Chairman of the Editorial Committee.

The Call to Worship by trumpeters

The Prelude, orchestra or organ

Selected Hymns

The Doxology

Praise God, from Whom all Blessings flow

The Old Hundredth   L. M.

THOMAS KEN, 1709   LOUIS BOURGEOIS, *Genevan Psalter*, 1551

Praise God, from whom all bless-ings flow; Praise Him all crea-tures here be-low;

Praise Him a-bove, ye heavenly host; Praise Fa-ther, Son, and Ho-ly Ghost. A-men.

Dedicatory Introit

Chaplain: One thing have I desired of the Lord; that will I seek after: that I may dwell in the house of the Lord, to behold the beauty of the Lord, and to enquire in his temple.

People: For in the time of trouble shall He hide me in his pavilion: in the secret of his tabernacle shall He hide me.

Chaplain: How amiable are thy tabernacles, O Lord of hosts.

People: My soul longeth, yea, even fainteth for the courts of God.

Chaplain: Thus saith the Lord, The hour cometh and now is when the true worshipers shall worship the Father in spirit and in truth, for such doth the Father seek to worship Him.

People: **Our feet shall stand within thy gates, O Jerusalem.**

Chaplain: This is the house of the Lord: this is none other than the gate of heaven.

People: **The Lord is in his holy temple: let all the earth keep silence before Him.**

Unison: Almighty God, Who hast given us grace at this time with one accord to make our common supplications unto Thee, and dost promise that where two or three are gathered together in thy Name that Thou wilt grant their requests: fulfill now, O Lord, the desires and petitions of thy servants, as may be most expedient for them, granting us in this world knowledge of the truth, and in the world to come life everlasting. Amen.

Hymn of Praise

The Prayers which may include:

Prayer of General Confession in unison

Almighty and most merciful Father, we have erred, and strayed from thy ways like lost sheep. We have followed too much the devices and desires of our own hearts. We have offended against thy holy laws. We have left undone those things which we ought to have done; and we have done those things which we ought not to have done; and there is no health in us. But Thou, O Lord, have mercy upon us, miserable offenders. Spare Thou those, O God, who confess their faults. Restore Thou those who are penitent; according to thy promises declared unto mankind in Christ Jesus our Lord. And grant, O most merciful Father, for his sake, that we may hereafter live a godly, righteous, and sober life, to the glory of thy holy Name. Amen.

6

Prayer for Pardon

Prayer for Our Country

Almighty God, Who has given us this good land for our heritage, we humbly beseech Thee that we may always prove ourselves a people mindful of thy favor and glad to do thy will. Bless our land with honorable industry, sound learning, and pure manners. Save us from violence, discord, and confusion; from pride and arrogancy and from every evil way. Defend our liberties and fashion into one united people the multitudes brought hither out of many kindreds and tongues. Endue with the spirit of wisdom those to whom in thy Name we entrust the authority of government, that there may be justice and peace at home, and that through obedience to thy law, we may show forth thy praise among the nations of the earth.

In the time of prosperity fill our hearts with thankfulness, and in the day of trouble suffer not our trust in Thee to fail.

Through Jesus Christ our Lord. Amen.

The Lord's Prayer in unison

Our Father, Who art in heaven:

Hallowed be thy Name, thy kingdom come, thy will be done, on earth as it is in heaven.

Give us this day our daily bread. And forgive us our trespasses, as we forgive those who trespass against us. And lead us not into temptation, but deliver us from evil.

For thine is the kingdom, and the power, and the glory, for ever. Amen.

Hymn

Responsive Reading

The Gloria

Glory be to the Father

Gloria Patri

H. W. GREATOREX

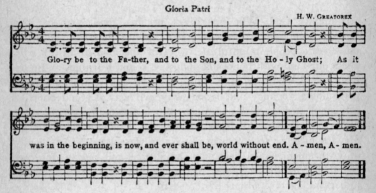

Glo-ry be to the Fa-ther, and to the Son, and to the Ho - ly Ghost; As it was in the beginning, is now, and ever shall be, world without end. A - men, A - men.

The Creed or other declaration of faith

I believe in God the Father Almighty, Maker of heaven and earth: and in Jesus Christ his only Son, our Lord; Who was conceived by the Holy Ghost; born of the virgin Mary, suffered under Pontius Pilate, was crucified, dead, and buried; He descended into hell; the third day He rose again from the dead; He ascended into heaven and sitteth on the right hand of God the Father Almighty; from thence He shall come to judge the quick and the dead. I believe in the Holy Ghost; the holy catholic church; the communion of saints; the forgiveness of sins; the resurrection of the body; and the life everlasting. Amen.

The Scripture

Special Music or a hymn

Sermon or Presentation of the Lesson

Hymn

Benediction

My Country, 'tis of Thee

America 6 6 4 6 6 6 4

SAMUEL F. SMITH, 1832   Anonymous, c. 1740

1. My coun - try, 'tis of thee, Sweet land of lib - er - ty,
Of thee I sing; Land where my fa - thers died, Land of the
pil - grim's pride, From eve - ry moun - tain side, Let free-dom ring. A-men.

Postlude

9

2 *Prayer for Purity of Thought*

Almighty God, unto Whom all hearts are open, all desires known, and from Whom no secrets are hid; cleanse the thoughts of our hearts by the inspiration of thy Holy Spirit, that we may perfectly love Thee, and worthily magnify thy holy Name. Through Jesus Christ our Lord. Amen.[1]

3 *A Prayer for a True Life*

Eternal God, Who committest to us the swift and solemn trust of life; since we know not what a day may bring forth, but only that the hour of serving Thee is always present, may we wake to the instant claims of thy holy will. Consecrate with thy presence the way our feet may go; and lift us above unrighteous anger and mistrust into faith and hope and charity. In all things draw us to the mind of Christ, that thy lost image may be traced again in us, to the glory of thy holy Name. Amen.

4 *A Prayer for Loved Ones*

O God, the Protector and Helper of all thy children, the Comfort and the Stay of the solitary, and those who are separated from those they love, we commit unto Thee and thy fatherly keeping our loved ones, beseeching Thee to grant unto them every good gift for the body and the soul, and to unite us all, present and absent, in true faith and love. Through Jesus Christ our Lord. Amen.

5 *A Sabbath Prayer*

In thy wisdom and justice, O Father, Thou hast given to us this special day in which to rest, to enjoy our beautiful world, to think of Thee and all whom Thou dost love. Forgive us, we pray Thee, that so often in carelessness and selfishness we forget Thee. On this Holy Day speak to our hearts and help us to remember the countless blessings Thou hast prepared for our good. Forbid that through our selfishness the day should be hard for others. Accept, we pray, the worship of loving hearts and devotion of daily lives in which we remember others and forget ourselves. Through Christ our Lord. Amen.

1 Gregorian Sacramentary, A.D. 590.

Grant us, O Lord, to pass this day in gladness and peace, without stumbling and without stain; that, reaching the eventide victorious over all temptation, we may praise Thee, the Eternal God, who art blessed forever, and dost hold in thy hand the destinies of the visible creation, world without end. Through Christ our Lord. Amen.

7   *Evening Prayer*

O Lord, support us all the day long of this troublous life, until the shadows lengthen, and the evening comes, and the busy world is hushed, and the fever of life is over, and our work is done. Then of thy great mercy grant us a safe lodging, and a holy rest, and peace at last. Through Jesus Christ our Lord. Amen.

8   *A Prayer for Mother*

Lord Jesus, Thou hast known a mother's love and tender care, and Thou wilt hear while for my own mother most dear I make this Sabbath prayer. Protect her life, I pray, who gave the gift of life to me; and may she know from day to day, the deepening glow of joy that comes from Thee. I cannot pay my debt for all the love that she has given; but Thou, Love's Lord, wilt not forget her due reward—Bless her in earth and heaven. Amen.[1]

9   *General Supplication*

Almighty God, Who hast given us grace at this time with one accord to make our common supplications unto Thee; and dost promise that where two or three are gathered together in thy Name Thou wilt grant their requests; fulfill now, O Lord, the desires and petitions of thy servants, as may be most expedient for them; granting us in this world knowledge of the truth, and in the world to come life everlasting. Amen.[2]

---

1 Henry Van Dyke.
2 St. Chrysostom (Circa 347-407).

Father Everlasting, Who hast set us in the fellowship of thy Son Jesus Christ, be near to us in this hour of solemn meditation. May our hearts be open to every holy affection, and ready to receive and cherish every sacred memory and sacred impression. Give us to know the power of that death which this day commemorates. Let a portion of the spirit which led our Saviour to the cross descend upon us and fill our hearts with the love of Thee and man. Here and now may every selfish passion and desire be quieted, and may that peace which passeth all understanding keep our hearts and minds in Christ Jesus. Amen.

11 *A Prayer of Thanksgiving*

Almighty God, Father of all mercies, we, thine unworthy servants, do give Thee most humble and hearty thanks, for all thy goodness and lovingkindness to us, and to all men; we bless Thee for our creation, preservation, and all the blessings of this life; but above all for thine inestimable love in the redemption of the world through our Lord Jesus Christ; for the means of grace, and for the hope of glory. And we beseech Thee, give us that due sense of all thy mercies, that our hearts may be unfeignedly thankful; and that we show forth thy praise, not only with our lips, but in our lives, by giving up ourselves to thy service, and walking before Thee in holiness and righteousness all our days: Through Jesus Christ our Lord, to Whom with Thee and the Holy Ghost, be all honor and glory, world without end. Amen.[1]

12 *A Prayer at Taps*

Before we go to rest we commit ourselves to thy care, O God our Father, beseeching Thee through Christ our Lord to keep alive thy grace in our hearts. Watch Thou, O Heavenly Father, with those who wake, or watch, or weep to-night, and give thine angels charge over those who sleep. Tend those who are sick, rest those who are weary, soothe those who suffer, pity those in affliction; be near and bless those who are dying, and keep under thy holy care those who are dear to us. Through Christ our Lord. Amen.

1 Edward Reynolds, 1661.

Almighty and most merciful Father, we have erred and strayed from thy ways like lost sheep. We have followed too much the devices and the desires of our own hearts. We have offended against thy holy laws. We have left undone those things which we ought to have done; and we have done those things which we ought not to have done; and there is no health in us. But Thou, O Lord, have mercy upon us, miserable offenders. Spare Thou those, O God, who confess their faults. Restore Thou those who are penitent, according to thy promises declared unto mankind in Christ Jesus our Lord. And grant, O most merciful Father, for his sake, that we may hereafter live a godly, righteous, and sober life, to the glory of thy holy Name. Amen.[1]

14   *A Prayer for Salvation*

Almighty God, teach us, we pray Thee, by blessed experience, to apprehend what was meant of old when Jesus Christ was called the power of God unto salvation, for we stand in need of salvation from sin, from doubt, from weakness, and from craven fear; we cannot save ourselves; we are creatures of a day, short-sighted, and too often driven about by every wind of passion and opinion. We need to be stayed upon a higher strength. We need to lay hold on Thee. Manifest Thyself unto us, our Father, as the Saviour of our souls, and deliver us from the bondage of corruption into the glorious liberty of the children of God. Amen.[2]

15   *The Lord's Prayer*

Our Father, Who art in heaven:

Hallowed be thy Name, thy kingdom come, thy will be done, on earth as it is in heaven.

Give us this day our daily bread. And forgive us our trespasses, as we forgive those who trespass against us. And lead us not into temptation, but deliver us from evil.

For thine is the kingdom, and the power, and the glory, for ever. Amen.

1 Based on the Latin of Valerand Pullain, 1551, and of John A. Lasco.
2 John Hunter.

I believe in God the Father Almighty, Maker of heaven and earth: and in Jesus Christ his only Son, our Lord; Who was conceived by the Holy Ghost; born of the virgin Mary, suffered under Pontius Pilate, was crucified, dead and buried; He descended into hell; the third day He rose again from the dead; He ascended into heaven and sitteth on the right hand of God the Father Almighty; from thence He shall come to judge the quick and the dead.

I believe in the Holy Ghost; the holy catholic church; the communion of saints; the forgiveness of sins; the resurrection of the body; and the life everlasting. Amen.

17   *The Declaration of Faith*

I believe in God our Father, infinite in wisdom, goodness, and love, and in his Son, our Saviour, the Lord Jesus Christ, Who for us men and our salvation lived and died and liveth evermore, exalted at the right hand of the Father, whose kingdom shall have no end.

And I believe in the Holy Spirit of God, the Lord and Giver of Life, proceeding from the Father and the Son, and with the Father and the Son exalted and glorified; taking of the things of Christ, revealing them to us; comforting, renewing, inspiring our spirits.

I believe in the persistence of personality and the immortality of the soul and I am resolved through the grace given unto me to order my life in the works of faith and in the ways of the holy commandments, looking for the victory of righteousness over evil, life over death, and for the life of the world to come. Amen.

I. Thou shalt have no other gods before Me.

II. Thou shalt not make unto thee any graven image, or any likeness of anything that is in heaven above, or that is in the earth beneath, or that is in the water under the earth: thou shalt not bow down thyself to them, nor serve them: for I the Lord thy God am a jealous God, visiting the iniquity of the fathers upon the children unto the third and fourth generation of them that hate Me; and showing mercy unto thousands of them that love Me, and keep my commandments.

III. Thou shalt not take the Name of the Lord thy God in vain; for the Lord will not hold him guiltless that taketh his Name in vain.

IV. Remember the Sabbath-day, to keep it holy. Six days shalt thou labor, and do all thy work: but the seventh day is the Sabbath of the Lord thy God; in it thou shalt not do any work, thou, nor thy son, nor thy daughter, thy man-servant, nor thy maid-servant, nor thy cattle, nor thy stranger that is within thy gates; for in six days the Lord made heaven and earth, the sea, and all that in them is, and rested the seventh day: wherefore the Lord blessed the Sabbath-day, and hallowed it.

V. Honor thy father and thy mother: that thy days may be long upon the land which the Lord thy God giveth thee.

VI. Thou shalt not kill.

VII. Thou shalt not commit adultery.

VIII. Thou shalt not steal.

IX. Thou shalt not bear false witness against thy neighbor.

X. Thou shalt not covet thy neighbor's house, thou shalt not covet thy neighbor's wife, nor his man-servant, nor his maid-servant, nor his ox, nor his ass, nor any thing that is thy neighbor's.

Chaplain   Proverbs 4

Enter not into the path of the wicked, and go not in the way of evil men. The way of the wicked is as darkness: but the path of the just is as the shining light, that shineth more and more unto the perfect day.

Chaplain and People   Psalm 1

Blessed is the man that walketh not in the counsel of the ungodly, nor standeth in the way of sinners:

Nor sitteth in the seat of the scornful.

But his delight is in the law of the Lord:

And in his law doth he meditate day and night.

And he shall be like a tree planted by the rivers of water:

That bringeth forth his fruit in his season.

His leaf also shall not wither:

And whatsoever he doeth shall prosper.

The ungodly are not so:

But are like the chaff which the wind driveth away.

Therefore the ungodly shall not stand in the judgment:

Nor sinners in the congregation of the righteous.

For the Lord knoweth the way of the righteous:

But the way of the ungodly shall perish.

Chaplain   Matthew 7   John 14

Enter ye in at the strait gate; for wide is the gate, and broad is the way, that leadeth to destruction, and many there be which go in thereat: because strait is the gate, and narrow is the way, which leadeth unto life, and few there be that find it.

I am the way, the truth, and the life: no man cometh unto the Father, but by Me.

Nos. 19-39 inclusive, Copyright 1941, Ivan L. Bennett.

Chaplain   Ecclesiastes 12

Remember now thy Creator in the days of thy youth, while the evil days come not, nor the years draw nigh, when thou shalt say, I have no pleasure in them; while the sun, or the light, or the moon, or the stars be not darkened; nor the clouds return after the rain. . . . For God shall bring every work into judgment, whether it be good, or whether it be evil.

Chaplain and People

Lord, how are they increased that trouble **me:**
    Many are they that rise up against me.
Many there be which say of my soul:
    There is no help for him in God.
But Thou, O Lord, art a shield for me:
    My glory, and the lifter up of mine head.
I cried unto the Lord with my voice:
    And He heard me out of his holy hill.
I laid me down and slept:
    I awaked; for the Lord sustained me.
I will not be afraid of ten thousands of people:
    That have set themselves against me round about.
Arise, O Lord:
    Save me, O my God.
Salvation belongeth unto the Lord:
    Thy blessing is upon thy people.

Chaplain   Romans 8

For I am persuaded, that neither death, nor life, nor angels, nor principalities, nor powers, nor things present, nor things to come, nor height, nor depth, nor any other creature, shall be able to separate us from the love of God, which is in Christ Jesus our Lord.

Chaplain   Isaiah 26

In the way of thy judgments, O Lord, have we waited for Thee; Thou wilt keep him in perfect peace, whose mind is stayed on Thee: because he trusteth in Thee.

Chaplain and People   Psalm 4

Hear me when I call, O God of my righteousness:

Thou hast enlarged me when I was in distress.

Have mercy upon me:

And hear my prayer.

O ye sons of men, how long will ye turn my glory into shame?

How long will ye love vanity, and seek after falsehood?

But know that the Lord hath set apart him that is godly for Himself:

The Lord will hear when I call unto Him.

Stand in awe, and sin not:

Commune with your own heart upon your bed, and be still.

Offer the sacrifices of righteousness:

And put your trust in the Lord.

There be many that say, Who will shew us any good?

Lord, lift Thou up the light of thy countenance upon us.

Thou hast put gladness in my heart:

More than in the time that their corn and wine increased.

I will both lay me down in peace, and sleep:

For Thou, Lord, only makest me dwell in safety.

Chaplain   Romans 8

As many as are led by the Spirit of God, they are the sons of God. The Spirit itself beareth witness with our spirit, that we are the children of God: and if children, then heirs; heirs of God and joint heirs with Christ; if so be that we suffer with Him that we may be also glorified together.

Chaplain Malachi 1

From the rising of the sun even unto the going down of the same my Name shall be great among the Gentiles; and in every place incense shall be offered unto my Name, and a pure offering: for my Name shall be great among the heathen, saith the Lord of Hosts.

Chaplain and People Psalm 8

O Lord, our Lord, how excellent is thy Name in all the earth:

Who hast set thy glory above the heavens.

Out of the mouth of babes and sucklings hast Thou ordained strength because of thine enemies:

That Thou mightest still the enemy and the avenger.

When I consider thy heavens, the work of thy fingers:

The moon and the stars, which Thou hast ordained:

What is man, that Thou art mindful of him:

And the son of man, that Thou visitest him?

For Thou hast made him a little lower than the angels:

And hast crowned him with glory and honor.

Thou madest him to have dominion over the works of thy hands:

Thou hast put all things under his feet;

All sheep and oxen:

Yea, and the beasts of the field;

The fowl of the air, and the fish of the sea:

And whatsoever passeth through the paths of the seas.

O Lord, our Lord:

How excellent is thy Name in all the earth!

Chaplain Exodus 20

Thou shalt not take the Name of the Lord thy God in vain; for the Lord will not hold him guiltless that taketh his Name in vain.

Chaplain Wisdom 4

In memory of virtue is immortality, because it is recognized both before God and before man: when it is present men imitate it, and they long after it when it is departed: and throughout all time it marches crowned in triumph, victorious in the strife for the prizes that are undefiled.

Chaplain and People Psalm 15

Lord, who shall abide in thy tabernacle:
  Who shall dwell in thy holy hill?
He that walketh uprightly and worketh righteousness:
  And speaketh the truth in his heart.
He that backbiteth not with his tongue, nor doeth evil to his neighbor:
  Nor taketh up a reproach against his neighbor.
In whose eyes a vile person is contemned, but he honoreth them that fear the Lord:
  He that sweareth to his own hurt, and changeth not.
He that putteth not out his money to usury: nor taketh reward against the innocent.
  He that doeth these things: shall never be moved.

Chaplain Micah 6 Psalm 112

He hath showed thee, O man, what is good; and what doth the Lord require of thee, but to do justly, and to love mercy, and to walk humbly with thy God?

Unto the upright there ariseth light in the darkness. It shall be well with the man that dealeth graciously. He shall maintain his cause in judgment. He shall not be afraid of evil tidings. The righteous shall be had in everlasting remembrance.

Chaplain   Psalm 119

Wherewithal shall a young man cleanse his way? By taking heed
thereto according to thy word. . . . O let me not wander from thy
commandments. Open Thou mine eyes that I may behold won-
drous things out of thy law.

Chaplain and People   Psalm 19

The law of the Lord is perfect, converting the soul:
The testimony of the Lord is sure, making wise the simple.
The statutes of the Lord are right, rejoicing the heart:
**The commandment of the Lord is pure, enlightening the
eyes.**
The fear of the Lord is clean, enduring forever:
**The judgments of the Lord are true and righteous alto-
gether.**
More to be desired are they than gold, yea, than much fine gold:
Sweeter also than honey and the honeycomb.
Moreover by them is thy servant warned:
And in keeping them there is great reward.
Who can understand his errors:
Cleanse Thou me from secret faults.
Keep back thy servant also from presumptuous sins; let them **not**
have dominion over me:
**Then shall I be upright, and I shall be innocent from the
great transgression.**
Let the words of my mouth, and the meditation of my heart be
acceptable in thy sight:
O Lord, my strength and my Redeemer.

Chaplain   Proverbs **3**

My son, forget not my law; but let thine heart keep my commandments: for length of days, and long life, and peace, shall
they add to thee. Let not mercy and truth forsake thee; bind them
about thy neck: write them upon the table of thine heart: so shalt
thou find favour and good understanding in the sight of God and
man.

Chaplain   Isaiah 40   Ezekiel 34

Thus saith the Lord God, As a shepherd seeketh out his flock in the day he is among his sheep that are scattered, so will I seek out my sheep and will deliver them out of the places where they have been scattered in the cloudy and dark day.

He will feed his flock like a shepherd; He will gather the lambs in his arms and carry them in his bosom, and will gently lead those that have their young.

Chaplain and People   Psalm 23

The Lord is my Shepherd:

I shall not want.

He maketh me to lie down in green pastures:

He leadeth me beside the still waters.

He restoreth my soul:

He leadeth me in the paths of righteousness for his Name's sake.

Yea, though I walk through the valley of the shadow of death, I will fear no evil:

For Thou art with me, thy rod and thy staff they comfort me.

Thou preparest a table before me in the presence of mine enemies:

Thou anointest my head with oil, my cup runneth over.

Surely goodness and mercy shall follow me all the days of my life:

And I will dwell in the house of the Lord for ever.

Chaplain   John 10

I am the good Shepherd, and know my sheep, and am known of mine. My sheep hear my voice, and I know them, and they follow Me: and I give unto them eternal life; and they shall never perish, neither shall any man pluck them out of my hand. My Father which gave them to Me is greater than all: and no man is able to pluck them out of my Father's hand.

Chaplain Isaiah 32

Behold a king shall reign in righteousness and princes shall rule in justice: and a man shall be as a hiding place from the wind, and a covert from the tempest, as rivers of water in a dry place, the shade of a great rock in a weary land. And the eyes of them that see shall not be dim, and the ears of them that hear shall hearken; the heart of the rash shall understand knowledge, and the tongue of the stammerer shall speak plainly.

Chaplain and People Psalm 24

The earth is the Lord's, and the fulness thereof:

The world, and they that dwell therein.

Who shall ascend into the hill of the Lord:

Or who shall stand in his holy place?

He that hath clean hands, and a pure heart:

Who hath not lifted up his soul unto vanity, nor sworn deceitfully.

He shall receive the blessing from the Lord.

And righteousness from the God of his salvation.

Lift up your heads, O ye gates, and be ye lifted up, ye everlasting doors:

And the King of Glory shall come in.

Who is this King of Glory?

The Lord strong and mighty, the Lord mighty in battle.

Lift up your heads, O ye gates, even lift them up ye everlasting doors:

And the King of Glory shall come in.

Who is this King of Glory?

The Lord of hosts, He is the King of Glory.

Chaplain Revelation 19

And I saw heaven opened, and behold, a white horse; and He that sat thereon was called Faithful and True and in righteousness He doth judge and make war.... And He was clothed in vesture dipped in blood: and his Name is called the Word of God.... And He hath on his vesture and on his thigh a name written, King of Kings and Lord of Lords.

Chaplain

Hast thou not known? Hast thou not heard? The everlasting
God, the Lord, the Creator of the ends of the earth, fainteth not,
neither is weary; there is no searching of his understanding. He
giveth power to the faint; and to him that hath no might He in-
creaseth strength.

Chaplain and People   Psalm 25

Unto Thee, O Lord, do I lift up my soul:

O my God, I trust in Thee: let me not be ashamed.

Yea, let none that wait on Thee be ashamed:

Show me thy ways, O Lord: teach me thy paths.

Lead me in thy truth, and teach me: for Thou art the God of my
salvation:

On Thee do I wait all the day.

Remember, O Lord, thy tender mercies and thy lovingkindness:

For they have been ever of old.

The troubles of my heart are enlarged:

O bring Thou me out of my distresses.

Look upon mine afflictions and my pain:

And forgive all my sins.

O keep my soul, and deliver me: let me not be ashamed:

For I put my trust in Thee.

Let integrity and uprightness preserve me:

For I wait on Thee.

Chaplain   Timothy 6

Fight the good fight of faith, lay hold on eternal life, whereunto
thou art called and hast professed before many witnesses the good
profession. I give thee charge in the sight of God, Who quick-
eneth all things, and before Jesus Christ, that thou keep this commandment without spot, unrebukable, until the appearing of our
Lord Jesus Christ.

Chaplain   Isaiah 55

Seek ye the Lord while He may be found, call ye upon Him while He is near: let the wicked forsake his way, and the unrighteous man his thoughts: and let him return unto the Lord, and He will have mercy upon him; and to our God, for He will abundantly pardon.

Chaplain and People   Psalm 27

Hear, O Lord, when I cry with my voice:

Have mercy also upon me, and answer me.

When Thou saidst, Seek ye my face:

My heart said unto Thee, Thy face, Lord, will I seek.

Hide not thy face far from me:

Put not thy servant away in anger.

Thou hast been my help:

Leave me not, neither forsake me, O God of my salvation.

When my father and my mother forsake me:

Then the Lord will take me up.

Teach me thy way, O Lord:

And lead me in a plain path, because of mine enemies.

Deliver me not over unto the will of mine enemies:

For false witnesses are risen up against me, and such as breathe out cruelty.

I had fainted unless I had believed to see the goodness of the Lord in the land of the living.

Wait on the Lord, be of good courage, and He shall strengthen thine heart: Wait, I say, on the Lord.

Chaplain   Luke 19

Jesus saith...The Son of Man is come to seek and to save that which was lost.

John 3

For God sent not his Son into the world to condemn the world; but that the world through Him might be saved.

Chaplain　　　　　　　　　　　　　　　　　　　Isaiah 60

Arise, shine; for thy light is come, and the glory of the Lord is risen upon thee. For, behold, darkness shall cover the earth and gross darkness the people: but the Lord shall arise upon thee, and his glory shall be seen upon thee. . . . Thy sun shall no more go down; neither shall thy moon withdraw itself: for the Lord shall be thine everlasting Light.

Chaplain and People　　　　　　　　　　　　　　Psalm 27

The Lord is my Light and my Salvation, whom shall I fear?

The Lord is the strength of my life, of whom shall I be afraid?

Though an host should encamp against me, my heart shall not fear:

Though war should rise against me, in this will I be confident:

One thing have I desired of the Lord, that will I seek after:

That I may dwell in the house of the Lord all the days of my life, to behold the beauty of the Lord, and to enquire in his temple.

For in the time of trouble He shall hide me in his pavilion:

In the secret of his tabernacle shall He hide me.

He shall set me up upon a rock:

And now shall mine head be lifted up above mine enemies round about me.

Therefore will I offer in his tabernacle sacrifices of joy:

I will sing, yea, I will sing praises unto the Lord.

Chaplain　　　　　　　　　　　　　　　　　　　John 8

I am the Light of the World: he that followeth Me shall not walk in darkness, but shall have the light of life.

　　　　　　　　　　　　　　　　　　　　　　　John 12

Yet a little while is the light with you. Walk while ye have the light, lest darkness come upon you. . . . While ye have the light, believe in the light, that ye may be children of the light.

Chaplain   Te Deum Laudamus

We praise Thee, O God; we acknowledge Thee to be the Lord. All the earth doth worship Thee, the Father everlasting. To Thee all angels cry aloud; the heavens and all the powers therein; to Thee cherubim and seraphim continually do cry,—Holy, Holy, Holy, Lord God of Sabaoth: Heaven and earth are full of the majesty of thy glory.

Chaplain and People   Psalm 34

I will bless the Lord at all times:

His praise shall continually be in my mouth.

My soul shall make her boast in the Lord:

The humble shall hear thereof and be glad.

O magnify the Lord with me:

And let us exalt his Name together.

I sought the Lord, and He heard me:

And delivered me from all my fears.

This poor man cried, and the Lord heard him:

And saved him out of all his troubles.

The Angel of the Lord encampeth round about **them that fear** Him:

And delivereth them.

O taste and see that the Lord is good:

Blessed is the man that trusteth in Him.

O fear the Lord, ye his saints:

For there is no want to them that fear Him.

Chaplain   Romans 8

For we know that all things work together for good to them that love God, to them that are the called according to his purpose.

Chaplain   Ecclesiastes 12

Fear God and keep his commandments: for this is the whole duty of man. For God shall bring every work into judgment, with every secret thing, whether it be good, or whether it be evil.

Chaplain and People   Psalm 24

Come, ye children, hearken unto me:

I will teach you the fear of the Lord.

What man is he that desireth life:

And loveth many days, that he may see good?

Keep thy tongue from evil:

And thy lips from speaking guile.

Depart from evil, and do good:

Seek peace, and pursue it.

The eyes of the Lord are upon the righteous:

And his ears are open unto their cry.

The face of the Lord is against them that do evil:

To cut off the remembrance of them from the earth.

The Lord is nigh unto them that are of a broken heart:

And saveth such as be of a contrite spirit.

Many are the afflictions of the righteous:

But the Lord delivereth him out of them all.

The Lord redeemeth the soul of his servants:

And none of them that trust in Him shall be desolate.

Chaplain   Proverbs 9

The fear of the Lord is the beginning of wisdom: and the knowledge of the holy is understanding. For by wisdom thy days shall be multiplied, and the years of thy life increased.

Chaplain   Isaiah 40

O thou that tellest good tidings to Zion, get thee up into the high
mountain; O thou that tellest good tidings to Jerusalem, lift up
thy voice with strength; lift it up, be not afraid; say unto the
cities of Judah, Behold your God!

Chaplain and People   Isaiah 9

The people that walked in darkness have seen a great light:

> They that dwelt in the land of the shadow of death, upon
> them hath the light shined.

For unto us a child is born,

> Unto us a son is given;

And the government shall be upon his shoulder:

> And his name shall be called Wonderful, Counsellor,
> Mighty God, Everlasting Father, Prince of Peace.

Of the increase of his government and of peace there shall be no
end,

> Upon the throne of David, and upon his kingdom, to
> establish it,

And to uphold it with justice and with righteousness from hence-
forth even forever.

> The zeal of the Lord of hosts will perform this.

Chaplain   Luke 2

And there were in the same country shepherds abiding in the
field, keeping watch over their flock by night. And lo, the angel
of the Lord came upon them, and the glory of the Lord shone
round about them: and they were sore afraid. And the angel
said unto them, Fear not; for behold, I bring you glad tidings of
great joy which shall be to all people. For unto you is born this
day in the city of David a Saviour, which is Christ the Lord. . . .
And suddenly there was with the angel a multitude of the
heavenly host praising God, and saying, Glory to God in the
highest, and on earth peace, good will toward men.

Chaplain   Psalm 107

O give thanks unto the Lord, for He is good: for his mercy endureth forever. Let the redeemed of the Lord say so, whom He hath redeemed from the hand of the enemy. They wandered in the wilderness in a solitary way; they found no city to dwell in: hungry and thirsty their soul fainted in them. Then they cried unto the Lord in their trouble, and He delivered them out of their distresses.

Chaplain and People   Psalm 89

I will sing of the mercies of the Lord for ever:

  With my mouth will I make known thy faithfulness to all generations.

For I have said, Mercy shall be built up for ever:

  Thy faithfulness shalt Thou establish in the very heavens.

And the heavens shall praise thy wonders, O Lord:

  Thy faithfulness also in the congregations of the saints.

Thou rulest the raging of the sea:

  When the waves thereof arise, Thou stillest them.

The heavens are thine, the earth also is thine:

  As for the world and the fulness thereof, Thou hast founded them.

Justice and judgment are the habitation of thy throne:

  Mercy and truth shall go before thy face.

The Lord is our defense:

  And the Holy One of Israel is our King.

Chaplain   Psalm 66

I will go into thy house with burnt offerings: I will pay my vows, which my lips have uttered, and my mouth hath spoken, when I was in trouble. Blessed be God Who hath not turned away my prayer, nor his mercy from me.

Chaplain Psalm 33

Our soul waiteth for the Lord: He is our help and our shield. For our heart shall rejoice in Him, because we have trusted in his holy Name. Let thy mercy, O Lord, be upon us, according as we hope in Thee.

Chaplain and People Psalm 62

Truly my soul waiteth upon God:

From Him cometh my salvation.

He only is my rock and my salvation:

He is my defense, I shall not be greatly moved.

My soul, wait thou only upon God:

For my expectation is from Him.

In God is my salvation and my glory:

The rock of my strength, and my refuge, is in God.

Trust in Him at all times, ye people:

Pour out your heart before Him; God is a refuge for us.

Trust not in oppression, and become not vain in robbery:

If riches increase, set not your heart upon them.

God hath spoken once, twice have I heard this:

That power belongeth unto God.

Also unto Thee, O Lord, belongeth mercy:

For Thou renderest to every man according to his works.

Chaplain Luke 2

There was a man in Jerusalem whose name was Simeon, and the same was just and devout, waiting for the consolation of Israel, and it was revealed unto him by the Holy Ghost, that he should not see death, before he had seen the Lord's Christ. And he came by the Spirit into the temple: and when the parents brought in the child Jesus, to do for Him after the custom of the law, then took he Him up in his arms and blessed God, and said: Now lettest Thou thy servant depart in peace, according to thy word: for mine eyes have seen thy salvation which Thou hast prepared before the face of all people.

Chaplain Job 5

Behold, happy is the man whom God correcteth: Therefore despise not thou the chastening of the Almighty. For He maketh sore, and He bindeth up; He woundeth and his hands make whole. He shall deliver thee in six troubles; yea, in seven there shall no evil touch thee.

Chaplain and People Psalm 63

O God, Thou art my God:

> **Early will I seek Thee.**

My soul thirsteth for Thee:

> **My flesh longeth for Thee in a dry and thirsty land, where no water is;**

To see thy power and thy glory:

> **So I have seen Thee in the sanctuary.**

Because thy lovingkindness is better than life:

> **My lips shall praise Thee.**

Thus will I bless Thee while I live:

> **I will lift up my hands in thy Name.**

My soul shall be satisfied as with marrow and fatness:

> **And my mouth shall praise Thee with joyful lips;**

When I remember Thee upon my bed:

> **And meditate on Thee in the night watches.**

Because Thou hast been my help:

> **Therefore in the shadow of thy wings will I rejoice.**

My soul followeth hard after Thee:

> **Thy right hand upholdeth me.**

Chaplain Psalm 36

Trust in the Lord, and do good; delight thyself also in the Lord; and He shall give thee the desires of thine heart. Commit thy way unto the Lord; trust also in Him; and He shall bring it to pass.

Chaplain Venite

O come, let us sing unto the Lord: let us heartily rejoice in the strength of our salvation. Let us come before his presence with thanksgiving: and show ourselves glad in Him with psalms.

Chaplain and People Psalm 67

God be merciful unto us, and bless us:

And cause his face to shine upon us.

That thy way may be known upon earth:

Thy saving health among all nations.

Let the people praise Thee, O God:

Let all the people praise Thee.

O let the nations be glad and sing for joy:

For Thou shalt judge the people righteously, and govern the nations upon earth.

Let the people praise Thee, O God:

Let all the people praise Thee.

Then shall the earth yield her increase:

And God, even our own God, shall bless us.

God shall bless us:

And all the ends of the earth shall fear Him.

Chaplain Deuteronomy 8

Beware lest thou forget the Lord thy God, in not keeping his commandments; lest, when thou hast eaten and art full, and hast built goodly houses, and dwelt therein, and when thy herds, and thy flocks are multiplied, and all that thou hast is multiplied; then thy heart be lifted up, and thou forget the Lord thy God; lest, thou say, My power and the might of n.y hand hath gotten me this wealth. Thou shalt remember the Lord thy God, for it is He that giveth thee the power to get wealth.

Chaplain   Jubilate Deo

O go your way into his gates with thanksgiving and into his
courts with praise: be thankful unto Him, and speak ye good
of his Name. For the Lord is gracious, his mercy is everlasting:
and his truth endureth from generation to generation.

Chaplain and People   Psalm 95

O come let us sing unto the Lord:

Let us make a joyful noise to the Rock of our salvation.

Let us come before his presence with thanksgiving:

And make a joyful noise unto Him with psalms.

For the Lord is a great God:

And a great King above all gods.

In his hand are the deep places of the earth:

The strength of the hills is his also.

The sea is his, and He made it:

And his hands formed the dry land.

O come, let us worship and bow down:

Let us kneel before the Lord our Maker.

For He is our God and we are the people of his pasture:

And the sheep of his hand.

Today if ye will hear his voice:

Harden not your heart.

Chaplain   Revelation 21

Behold, the tabernacle of God is with men, and He shall dwell
with them, and they shall be his people, and God Himself shall
be with them and be their God: And He shall wipe away every
tear from their eyes; and death shall be no more; and neither
shall there be mourning, nor crying, nor pain any more: the first
things are passed away.

Chaplain   Wisdom 3

The souls of the righteous are in the hands of God, and no torment shall touch them. In the eyes of the foolish they seem to have died; and their departure is accounted to be their hurt; and their journeying away to be their ruin; but they are in peace. Their hope is the fulness of immortality.

Chaplain and People   ❧ Psalm 130

Out of the depths: have I cried unto Thee, O Lord:

Lord, hear my voice: let thine ears be attentive to the voice of my supplications.

If Thou, Lord, shouldest mark iniquities:

O Lord, who shall stand?

But there is forgiveness with Thee:

That Thou mayest be feared.

I wait for the Lord, my soul doth wait:

And in his word do I hope.

My soul waiteth for the Lord more than they that watch for the morning:

I say, more than they that watch for the morning.

Let Israel hope in the Lord, for with the Lord there is mercy and with Him is plenteous redemption:

And He shall redeem Israel from all his iniquities.

Chaplain   John 14

Let not your heart be troubled; ye believe in God, believe also in Me. In my Father's house are many mansions: if it were not so, I would have told you. I go to prepare a place for you. And if I go and prepare a place for you, I will come again, and receive you unto Myself; that where I am, there ye may be also.

Chaplain   Gloria in Excelsis

Glory be to God on high, and on earth peace, good-will toward men! We praise Thee, we bless Thee, we worship Thee, we glorify Thee, we give thanks to Thee for thy great glory, O Lord God, heavenly King. God the Father Almighty!

Chaplain and People   Luke 1

My soul doth magnify the Lord, and my spirit hath rejoiced in God my Saviour.

For He hath looked upon the low estate of his handmaid: For behold, from henceforth all generations shall call me blessed.

For He that is mighty hath done to me great things; and holy is his Name.

And his mercy is unto generations and generations of them that fear Him.

He hath showed strength with his arm; He hath scattered the proud in the imagination of their heart.

He hath put down princes from their thrones, and hath exalted them of low degree.

The hungry He hath filled with good things; and the rich He hath sent empty away.

He hath given help to Israel his servant, that he might remember mercy,

As He spake unto our fathers, to Abraham and his seed for ever.

Chaplain   Benedictus

Blessed be the Lord God of Israel: for He hath visited and re-deemed his people, and hath raised up a horn of salvation for us in the house of his servant David; as He spake by the mouth of his holy prophets, which have been since the world began: that we should be saved from our enemies and from the hand of all that hate us.

40   Mass of Christ the King

Prayers at Foot of Altar

In the name of the Father, and of the Son, and of the Holy Ghost. Amen.

Priest: I will go unto the Altar of God.

Response: **To God, who giveth joy to my youth.**

P.: Judge me, O God, and distinguish my cause from the nation that is not holy: deliver me from the unjust and deceitful man.

R.: **For Thou, O God, art my strength: why hast Thou cast me off? and why do I go sorrowful while the enemy afflicteth me?**

P.: Send forth Thy light and Thy truth: they have led me and brought me to Thy holy mount, and into Thy tabernacles.

R.: **And I will go unto the Altar of God: to God, who giveth joy to my youth.**

P.: I will praise Thee on the harp, O God, my God: why art thou sad, O my soul, and why dost thou disquiet me?

R.: **Hope thou in God, for I will yet praise Him: who is the salvation of my countenance, and my God.**

P.: Glory be to the Father, and to the Son, and to the Holy Ghost.

R.: **As it was in the beginning, is now, and ever shall be, world without end. Amen.**

P.: I will go unto the Altar of God.

R.: **Unto God, who giveth joy to my youth.**

P.: Our help is in the name of the Lord.

R.: **Who hath made heaven and earth.**

P.: I confess to Almighty God, to blessed Mary ever Virgin, to blessed Michael the Archangel, to blessed John the Baptist, to the holy Apostles Peter and Paul, and to all the Saints, that I have sinned exceedingly in thought, word, and deed, through my fault, through my fault, through my most grievous fault.

Therefore I beseech the blessed Mary ever Virgin, blessed Michael the Archangel, blessed John the Baptist, the holy Apostles Peter and Paul, and all the Saints, to pray to the Lord our God for me.

R.: **May Almighty God have mercy upon thee, and forgive thee thy sins, and bring thee unto life everlasting.**

P.: Amen.

P.: May Almighty God have mercy upon you, and forgive you your sins, and bring you unto life everlasting.

R.: **Amen.**

P.: May the Almighty and merciful Lord grant us pardon, absolution, and remission of our sins.

R.: **Amen.**

P.: Thou shalt turn again, O God, and quicken us.

R.: **And Thy people shall rejoice in Thee.**

P.: Show us Thy mercy, O Lord.

R.: **And grant us Thy salvation.**

P.: O Lord, hear my prayer.

R.: **And let my cry come unto Thee.**

P.: The Lord be with you.

R.: **And with thy spirit.**

Prayers Ascending Altar

P.: Take away from us our iniquities, we beseech Thee, O Lord: that we may be worthy to enter with pure minds into the Holy of Holies. Through Christ our Lord. Amen.

We beseech Thee, O Lord, by the merits of Thy Saints whose relics are here, and of all the Saints that Thou wouldst vouchsafe to forgive me all my sins. Amen.

Introit

The Lamb that was slain is worthy to receive power and divinity and wisdom and strength and honour; to Him be glory and empire for ever and ever. Ps. Give to the King, O God, Thy justice, and to the King's Son Thy judgement. Glory be....

Kyrie Eleison

P.: Lord, have mercy,

R.: **Lord, have mercy,**

P.: Lord, have mercy,

R.: **Christ, have mercy,**

P.: Christ, have mercy,

R.: **Christ, have mercy,**

P.: Lord, have mercy,

R.: **Lord, have mercy,**

P.: Lord, have mercy.

Gloria in Excelsis

Glory be to God on high, and on earth peace to men of good will. We praise Thee; we bless Thee; we worship Thee; we glorify Thee. We give Thee thanks for Thy great glory, O Lord God, heavenly King, God the Father Almighty. O Lord, the Only-begotten Son, Jesus Christ; O Lord God, Lamb of God, Son of the Father, who takest away the sins of the world, have mercy on us: Thou who takest away the sins of the world, receive our prayer; Thou who sittest at the right hand of the Father, have mercy on us. For Thou only art holy; Thou only art the Lord: Thou only, O Jesus Christ, with the Holy Ghost, art most high in the glory of God the Father. Amen.

Collects

1. Almighty everlasting God, who in Thy beloved Son, King of the whole world, hast willed to restore all things anew; grant in Thy mercy that all the families of nations, rent asunder by the wound of sin, may be subjected to His most gentle rule. Who with Thee liveth.

2. *Prayer for Peace:*

O God, from whom all holy desires, all right counsels and all just works do proceed; give to Thy servants that peace which the world cannot give; that our hearts may be disposed to obey Thy commandments, and the fear of enemies being removed, our times, by Thy protection, may be peaceful. Through our Lord.

Epistle

Lesson from the Epistle of blessed Paul the Apostle to the Colossians. Brethren: Giving thanks to God the Father, who hath made us worthy to be partakers of the lot of the saints in light: who hath delivered us from the power of darkness, and hath transferred us into the kingdom of the Son of His love, in whom we have redemption through His blood, the remission of sins; who is the image of the invisible God, the first born of every creature: for in Him were all things created in heaven and on earth, visible and invisible, whether thrones, or dominations, or principalities, or powers. All things were created by Him and in Him; and He is before all, and by Him all things consist. And He is the head of the body the Church, who is the beginning, the first-born from the dead, that in all things, He may hold the primacy: because in Him, it hath well pleased the Father that all fulness should dwell; and through Him to reconcile all things unto Himself, making peace through the blood of His cross, both as to the things on earth, and the things that are in heaven, in Jesus Christ our Lord.

Gospel

Continuation of the holy Gospel according to St. John. At that time: Pilate said to Jesus: Art Thou the King of the Jews? Jesus answered: Sayest thou this thing of thyself, or have others told it thee of Me? Pilate answered: Am I a Jew? Thine own nation and the chief priests have delivered Thee up to me: what hast Thou done? Jesus answered: My kingdom is not of this world. If My kingdom were of this world, My servants would certainly strive that I should not be delivered to the Jews; but now My kingdom is not from hence. Pilate therefore said to Him: Art thou a King then? Jesus answered: Thou sayest that I am a King. For this was I born, and for this came I into the world, that I should give testimony to the truth. Every one that is of the truth, heareth My voice.

Credo

I believe in one God, the Father Almighty, maker of heaven and earth, and of all things visible and invisible. And in one Lord Jesus Christ, the only begotten Son of God, born of the Father before all ages. God of God; Light of Light; true God of true God; begotten, not made; consubstantial to the Father, by whom all things were made. Who for us men, and for our salvation, came down from heaven, and was incarnate by the Holy Ghost, of the Virgin Mary: AND WAS MADE MAN. Was crucified also for us, suffered under Pontius Pilate, and was buried; and the third day He rose again, according to the scriptures. And ascended into heaven, sitteth at the right hand of the Father, and he shall come again with glory to judge both the living and the dead: of whose kingdom there shall be no end.—And I believe in the Holy Ghost, the Lord and Giver of Life, who proceedeth from the Father and the Son: who together with the Father and the Son is adored and glorified: who spake by the Prophets. And one holy Catholic and Apostolic Church. I confess one baptism for the remission of sins. And I look for the resurrection of the dead, and the life of the world to come. Amen.

Offertory

Ask of Me and I will give thee the nations for thine inheritance, and the ends of the earth for thy possession.

Secreta

1. We offer Thee, O Lord, the victim of man's reconciliation; grant, we beseech Thee, that He whom we immolate in our present sacrifices may Himself bestow on all nations the gifts of unity and peace. Who with Thee liveth and reigneth.

For Peace

2. O God, who sufferest not the nations who believe in Thee to be overwhelmed by any peril; vouchsafe to receive the prayers

and offerings of Thy servants, that in Thy mercy Thou wouldst grant peace to Christendom and make them secure against all their enemies. Through our Lord.

Preface

It is truly meet and just, right and availing unto salvation that we should at all times and in all places give thanks unto Thee, O holy Lord, Father Almighty and Everlasting God. Who with the oil of gladness hast anointed Thine only-begotten Son, our Lord Jesus Christ, as eternal High Priest and universal King; that offering Himself on the altar of the Cross as an immaculate host and peace-offering, He might complete the mysteries of human redemption; and all creation being made subject to His dominion, He might deliver into the hands of Thine infinite Majesty a kingdom eternal and universal, a kingdom of truth and life, a kingdom of holiness and grace, a kingdom of justice, love and peace. And therefore with the angels and archangels, with the thrones and dominions, and with all the heavenly hosts, we sing a hymn to Thy glory, saying without ceasing:

Sanctus

Holy, Holy, Holy, Lord God of Hosts. Heaven and earth are full of Thy glory. Hosanna in the highest. Blessed is he who cometh in the name of the Lord. Hosanna in the highest.

Canon of Mass

We, therefore, humbly pray and beseech Thee, most merciful Father, through Jesus Christ, Thy Son, our Lord, That Thou wouldst vouchsafe to accept and bless these gifts, these presents, these holy unspotted sacrifices, which in the first place, we offer Thee for Thy holy Catholic Church: which vouchsafe to grant peace, as also to preserve, unite, and govern throughout the whole world, together with Thy servant N. our Pope; N. our Bishop; as also all orthodox believers and professors of the Catholic and Apostolic Faith.

The Commemoration of the Living

Be mindful, O Lord, of Thy servants, men and women, N. and N. (*Make commemoration of the living you intend to pray for.*) And of all here present, whose faith and devotion are known to Thee; for whom we offer, or who offer up to Thee this Sacrifice of praise for themselves and all pertaining to them, for the redemption of their souls, for the hope of their salvation and well-being, and who pay their vows unto Thee, the eternal God, living and true.

Communicating with, and honoring in the first place the memory, of the glorious ever Virgin Mary, Mother of our God and Lord Jesus Christ; as also of Thy blessed Apostles and Martyrs, Peter and Paul, Andrew, James, John, Thomas, James, Philip, Bartholomew, Matthew, Simon and Thadeus, Linus, Cletus, Clement, Xystus, Cornelius, Cyprian, Lawrence, Chrysogonus, John and Paul, Cosmas and Damian, and all Thy Saints; by whose merits and prayers grant that we may in all things be defended by the aid of Thy protection. Through the same Christ Our Lord. Amen.

We therefore beseech Thee, O Lord, graciously to accept this oblation of our servitude, as also of Thy whole family; and to dispose our days in Thy peace, preserve us from eternal damnation, and rank us in the number of Thine elect. Through Christ our Lord. Amen.

Which oblation do Thou, O God, vouchsafe in all respects to bless, approve, ratify, and accept; that it may be made for us the Body and Blood of Thy most beloved Son Jesus Christ our Lord.

Who, the day before He suffered, took bread into His holy and venerable hands, and with eyes lifted up towards heaven, unto Thee, O God, His Almighty Father, giving thanks to Thee, did bless, break, and give unto His disciples, saying: Take, and eat ye all of this. For this is my Body.

(*At the Elevation the bell is rung thrice.*)

In like manner after He had supped taking also this excellent chalice into His holy and venerable hands, giving Thee also thanks, He blessed and gave it to His disciples, saying: Take and drink ye all of this, FOR THIS IS THE CHALICE OF MY BLOOD OF THE NEW AND ETERNAL TESTAMENT, THE MYSTERY OF FAITH: WHICH SHALL BE SHED FOR YOU AND FOR MANY, TO THE REMISSION OF SINS. As often as ye do these things, ye shall do them in remembrance of Me.

(The bell rings thrice.)

Wherefore, O Lord, we Thy servants, as also Thy holy people, calling to mind the blessed passion of the same Christ, Thy Son, our Lord, His resurrection from the dead, and admirable ascension into heaven, offer unto Thy most excellent Majesty, of Thy gifts bestowed upon us, a pure Host, a holy Host, an unspotted Host, the holy Bread of eternal life, and Chalice of everlasting salvation.

Upon which vouchsafe to look with a propitious and serene countenance, and to accept them, as Thou wert graciously pleased to accept the gifts of Thy just servant Abel, and the sacrifice of our Patriarch Abraham, and that which Thy High Priest Melchisedech offered to Thee,—a holy sacrifice and unspotted victim.

We most humbly beseech Thee, Almighty God, to command these things to be carried by the hands of Thy holy Angels to Thy altar on high, in the sight of Thy divine Majesty, that as many as shall partake of the most sacred Body and Blood of Thy Son at this altar may be filled with every heavenly grace and blessing. Through the same Christ our Lord. Amen.

Commemoration of the Dead

Be mindful, O Lord, of Thy servants N. and N., who are gone before us with the sign of faith, and rest in the sleep of peace.

(Here particular mention is silently made of such of the Dead as are to be prayed for.)

To these, O Lord, and to all that sleep in Christ, grant, we beseech Thee, a place of refreshment, light and peace; through the same Christ our Lord. Amen.

Also, to us sinners, Thy servants, confiding in the multitude of Thy mercies, vouchsafe to grant some part and fellowship with Thy holy apostles and martyrs; with John, Stephen, Matthias, Barnabas, Ignatius, Alexander, Marcellinus, Peter, Felicitas, Perpetua, Agatha, Lucy, Agnes, Cecilia, Anastasia, and with all Thy saints, into whose company we beseech Thee to admit us, not in consideration of our merit, but of Thy own gratuitous pardon. Through Christ our Lord. By whom, O Lord, Thou dost always create, sanctify, quicken, bless, and give us all these good things. By Him, and with Him, and in Him, is to Thee, God the Father Almighty, in the unity of the Holy Ghost, all honor and glory.

P.: For ever and ever.

R.: **Amen.**

Let us pray.

Instructed by Thy saving precepts, and following Thy divine directions, we presume to say:

Our Father, who art in heaven, hallowed be Thy name: Thy kingdom come: Thy will be done on earth as it is in heaven. Give us this day our daily bread: and forgive us our trespasses, as we forgive those who trespass against us. And lead us not into temptation.

R.: **But deliver us from evil.**

P.: Amen.

Deliver us, we beseech Thee, O Lord, from all evils, past, present, and to come: and by the intercession of blessed and glorious Mary ever Virgin, Mother of God, together with Thy blessed Apostles Peter and Paul, and Andrew, and all the Saints, mercifully grant peace in our days: that, aided by the help of Thy mercy, we may be always free from sin, and secure from all disturbance. Through the same our Lord Jesus Christ, Thy Son, who liveth and reigneth with Thee in the unity of the Holy Ghost, God.

P.: World without end.

R.: **Amen.**

P.: May the peace of the Lord be always with you.

R.: **And with thy spirit.**

May this mingling and consecration of the Body and Blood of our Lord Jesus Christ be to us that receive it effectual to life everlasting. Amen.

Lamb of God, who takest away the sins of the world, have mercy on us.

Lamb of God, who takest away the sins of the world, have mercy on us.

Lamb of God, who takest away the sins of the world, grant us Thy peace.

O Lord Jesus Christ, who saidst to Thy Apostles, Peace I leave you, My peace I give you: regard not my sins, but the faith of Thy Church; and vouchsafe to grant her that peace and unity which is agreeable to Thy will: who livest and reignest God world without end. Amen.

O Lord Jesus Christ, Son of the living God, who, according to the will of Thy Father with the cooperation of the Holy Ghost, hast by Thy death given life to the world; deliver me by this Thy most sacred Body and Blood from all my iniquities and from all evils; and make me always adhere to Thy commandments, and suffer me never to be separated from Thee. Who livest and reignest with God the Father world without end. Amen.

Let not the participation of Thy body, O Lord Jesus Christ, which I, though unworthy, presume to receive, turn to my judgment and condemnation; but let it, through Thy mercy, become a safeguard and remedy, both of soul and body; who with God the Father, in the unity of the Holy Ghost, livest and reignest God forever and ever. Amen.

I will take the Bread of heaven, and will call upon the name of the Lord.

Lord, I am not worthy that Thou shouldest enter under my roof; but only say the word, and my soul shall be healed.

May the body of our Lord Jesus Christ preserve my soul unto life everlasting. Amen.

Communion

The Lord shall sit a King for ever: the Lord shall bless His people in peace.

Postcommunions

1. Having received the food of immortality, we beseech Thee, O Lord, that we who glory in our service under the standard of Christ the King, may be able to reign with Him forever in His heavenly abode. Who with Thee...

For Peace

2. O God, who sufferest not the nations who believe in Thee to be overwhelmed by any peril; vouchsafe to receive the prayers and offerings of Thy servants, that in Thy mercy thou wouldst grant peace to Christendom and make them secure against all their enemies. Through our Lord.

Blessing

May Almighty God; the Father, Son, and Holy Ghost bless you.

R.: Amen.

P.: The Lord be with you.

R.: And with thy spirit.

Last Gospel

P.: The beginning of the holy Gospel according to John.

R.: **Glory be to Thee, O Lord.**

P.: In the beginning was the Word, and the Word was with God, and the Word was God. This was in the beginning with God. All things were made through Him, and without Him was made nothing that was made; in Him was life, and the life was the light of men: and the light shineth in darkness, and the darkness did not comprehend it. There was a man sent from God, whose name was John. This one came for a witness, to testify concerning the light, that all might believe through him. He was not the light, but he was to testify concerning the light. The true Light, which enlighteneth every man, cometh into this world. He was in the world, and the world was made through Him, and the world knew Him not. He came to His own possessions, and His own people received Him not. But to as many as received Him He gave power to become children of God, to those who believe in His name, who are born not of blood, nor of the will of the flesh, nor of the will of man, but of God. AND THE WORD WAS MADE FLESH (*Here all kneel*), and dwelt among us; and we saw His glory, the glory as of the Only-begotten of the Father, full of grace and truth.

R.: **Thanks be to God.**

41   Way of the Cross

(Prayers and Devotions as Composed by St. Alphonsus Liguori, about 1761.)

All Prayers to be said aloud by the entire congregation.

After Fourteenth Station:
Say *five times* the Our Father, Hail Mary *and* Glory be to the Father, *in honor of the five wounds of Jesus Christ, and then one* Our Father, Hail Mary, *and* Glory be to the Father, *for the intentions of the Pope.*

Preparatory Prayer

(*To be said kneeling before the Altar*)

My Lord Jesus Christ, * Thou hast made this journey to die for me with love unutterable, * and I have so many times unworthily abandoned Thee; * but now I love Thee with my whole heart, * and because I love Thee, I repent sincerely for having ever offended Thee. * Pardon me, my God, * and permit me to accompany Thee on this journey. * Thou goest to die for love of me; * I wish also, my beloved Redeemer, to die for love of Thee. * My Jesus, I will live and die always united to Thee. *

First Station

JESUS IS CONDEMNED TO DEATH.

(Genuflect)

Priest: We adore Thee, O Christ and we bless Thee.

People: Because by Thy holy Cross Thou hast redeemed the world.

(100 days, Leo XIII, March 4, 1882.)

(Stand)

Priest: Consider how Jesus, after having been scourged and crowned with thorns, was unjustly condemned by Pilate to die on the Cross.

(Kneel)

People: My adorable Jesus, it was not Pilate, * no, it was my sins that condemned Thee to die. * I beseech Thee by the merits of this sorrowful journey, * to assist my soul in its journey towards eternity.* I love Thee, my beloved Jesus; * I love Thee more than myself; * I repent with my whole heart for having offended Thee. * Never permit me to separate myself from Thee again. * Grant that I may love Thee always; * and then do with me what Thou wilt. *

(Say) Our Father—Hail Mary—Glory, *or*

Jesus, for Thee I live, * Jesus, for Thee I die. *
Jesus, I am Thine in life and in death. Amen.

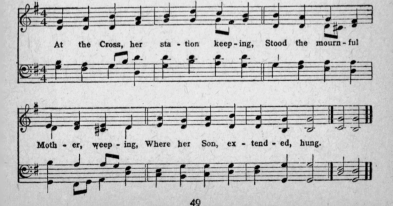

At the Cross, her sta-tion keep-ing, Stood the mourn-ful Moth-er, weep-ing, Where her Son, ex-tend-ed, hung.

Second Station

JESUS IS MADE TO BEAR HIS CROSS.

(Genuflect)

Priest: We adore Thee, O Christ and we bless Thee.

People: Because by Thy holy Cross Thou hast redeemed the world,

(Stand)

Priest: Consider how Jesus, in making this journey with the cross on His shoulders, thought of us, and offered for us to His Father the death He was about to undergo.

(Kneel)

People: My most beloved Jesus, * I embrace all the tribulations Thou hast destined for me until death. * I beseech Thee, * by the merits of the pain Thou didst suffer in carrying Thy Cross, * to give me the necessary help * to carry mine with perfect patience and resignation. * I love Thee, Jesus my Love; * I repent of having offended Thee. * Never permit me to separate myself from Thee again. * Grant that I may love Thee always; * and then do with me what Thou wilt. *

(Say) Our Father—Hail Mary—Glory, *or*

Jesus, for Thee I live, * Jesus, for Thee I die. *
Jesus, I am Thine in life and in death. Amen.

Through her Heart, His sor-row shar-ing All His bit-ter an-guish bear-ing, Now at length the sword has passed.

Third Station

JESUS FALLS THE FIRST TIME UNDER HIS CROSS.

(Genuflect)

Priest: We adore Thee, O Christ and we bless Thee.

People: Because by Thy Holy Cross Thou hast redeemed the world.

(Stand)

Priest: Consider this first fall of Jesus under His Cross, His flesh was torn by the scourges, His Head crowned with thorns, and He could scarcely walk, and yet He had to carry this great load upon His shoulders. The soldiers struck Him rudely, and thus He fell several times in His journey.

(Kneel)

People: My beloved Jesus, * it is not the weight of the Cross, but my sins, * which have made Thee suffer so much pain. * Ah, by the merits of this first fall, * deliver me from the misfortune of falling into mortal sin. * I love Thee, O my Jesus, with my whole heart; * I repent of having offended Thee. * Never permit me to offend Thee again. * Grant that I may love Thee always; * and then do with me what Thou wilt. *

(Say) Our Father—Hail Mary—Glory, *or*

Jesus, for Thee I live, * Jesus, for Thee I die. *
Jesus, I am Thine in life and in death. Amen.

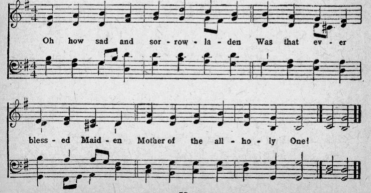

Oh how sad and sor-row-la-den Was that ev-er bless-ed Maid-en Mother of the all-ho-ly One!

Fourth Station

JESUS MEETS HIS AFFLICTED MOTHER.

(Genuflect)

Priest: We adore Thee, O Christ and we bless Thee.

People: Because by Thy Holy Cross Thou hast redeemed the world.

(Stand)

Priest: Consider the meeting of the Son and the Mother, which took place on this journey. Jesus and Mary looked at each other, and their looks became as so many arrows to wound those hearts which loved each other tenderly.

(Kneel)

People: My most loving Jesus, * by the sorrow Thou didst experience in this meeting, * grant me the grace of a truly devoted love for Thy most holy Mother. * And thou my Queen, * who wast overwhelmed with sorrow, * obtain for me by thy intercession * a continual and tender remembrance of the Passion of thy Son. * I love Thee, Jesus my Love; * I repent of ever having offended Thee. * Never permit me to offend Thee again. * Grant that I may love Thee; * and then do with me what Thou wilt. *

(Say) Our Father—Hail Mary—Glory, *or*

Jesus, for Thee I live, * Jesus, for Thee I die. *
Jesus, I am Thine in life and in death. Amen.

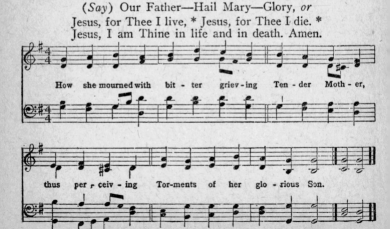

How she mourned with bit-ter griev-ing Ten-der Moth-er,

thus per-r ceiv-ing Tor-ments of her glo-rious Son.

Fifth Station

THE CYRENEAN HELPS JESUS TO CARRY HIS CROSS.

(Genuflect)

Priest: We adore Thee, O Christ and we bless Thee.

People: Because by Thy Holy Cross Thou hast redeemed the world.

(Stand)

Priest: Consider how the Jews, seeing that at each step Jesus was on the point of expiring, and fearing He would die on the way, when they wished Him to die the ignominious death of the Cross, constrained Simon the Cyrenean to carry the Cross behind our Lord.

(Kneel)

People: My most sweet Jesus, * I will not refuse the Cross, as the Cyrenean did; * I accept it, I embrace it. * I accept in particular the death Thou hast destined for me; * with all the pains that may accompany it; * I unite it to Thy death, I offer it to Thee. * Thou hast died for love of me; * I will die for love of Thee, and to please Thee. * Help me by Thy grace. * I love Thee, Jesus my Love; * I repent of having offended Thee. * Never permit me to offend Thee again. * Grant that I may love Thee; * and then do with me what Thou wilt. *

(Say) Our Father—Hail Mary—Glory, *or*
Jesus, for Thee I live, * Jesus, for Thee I die. *
Jesus, I am Thine in life and in death. Amen.

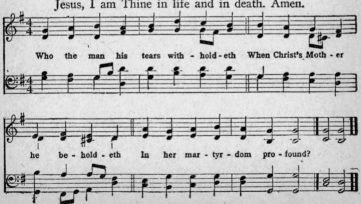

Who the man his tears with-hold-eth When Christ's Moth-er he be-hold-eth In her mar-tyr-dom pro-found?

Sixth Station

VERONICA WIPES THE FACE OF JESUS.

(Genuflect)

Priest: We adore Thee, O Christ and we bless Thee.

People: Because by Thy Holy Cross Thou hast redeemed the world.

(Stand)

Priest: Consider how the holy woman named Veronica, seeing Jesus so afflicted, and His face bathed in sweat and Blood, presented Him with a towel, with which He wiped His adorable Face, leaving on it the impression of His holy Countenance.

(Kneel)

People: My beloved Jesus, * Thy face was beautiful before, * but in this journey it has lost all its beauty, * and wounds and blood have disfigured it. * Alas, my soul also was once beautiful, * when it received Thy grace in Baptism; * but I have disfigured it since by my sins; * Thou alone, my Redeemer, canst restore it to its former beauty. * Do this by Thy Passion; * and then do with me what Thou wilt. *

(Say) Our Father—Hail Mary—Glory, *or*

Jesus, for Thee I live, * Jesus, for Thee I die. *
Jesus, I am Thine in life and in death. Amen.

Who not with com-pas-sion sat-ed Hath that Moth-er con-tem-plat-ed With her Son in sor-row bound?

Seventh Station

JESUS FALLS THE SECOND TIME.

(Genuflect)

Priest: We adore Thee, O Christ and we bless Thee.

People: Because by Thy Holy Cross Thou hast redeemed the world.

(Stand)

Priest: Consider the second fall of Jesus under the Cross—a fall which renews the pain of all the wounds of the Head and members of our afflicted Lord.

(Kneel)

People: My most gentle Jesus, * how many times hast Thou pardoned me, * and how many times have I fallen again, and begun again to offend Thee! * Oh, by the merits of this new fall, * give me the necessary help to persevere in Thy grace until death. * Grant that in all temptations which assail me * I may always commend myself to Thee. * I love Thee, Jesus my Love, with my whole heart; * I repent of having offended Thee. * Never permit me to offend Thee again. * Grant that I may love Thee always; * and then do with me what Thou wilt. *

(Say) Our Father—Hail Mary—Glory, *or*

Jesus, for Thee I live, * Jesus, for Thee I die. *
Jesus, I am Thine in life and in death. Amen.

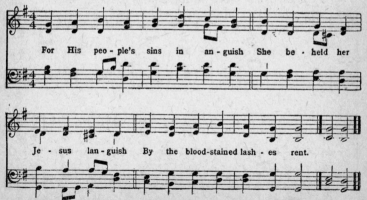

For His peo-ple's sins in an-guish She be-held her Je-sus lan-guish By the blood-stained lash-es rent.

Eighth Station

JESUS SPEAKS TO THE DAUGHTERS OF JERUSALEM.

(Genuflect)

Priest: We adore Thee, O Christ and we bless Thee.

People: Because by Thy Holy Cross Thou hast redeemed the world.

(Stand)

Priest: Consider how those women wept with compassion at seeing Jesus in such a pitiful state, streaming with Blood, as He walked along. But Jesus said to them, "Weep not for Me, but for your children."

(Kneel)

People: My Jesus, laden with sorrows, * I weep for the offences I have committed against Thee, * because of the pains they have deserved, * and still more because of the displeasure they have caused Thee, * who hast loved me so much. * It is Thy love, more than the fear of hell, * which causes me to weep for my sins. * My Jesus, I love Thee more than myself; * I repent of having offended Thee. * Never permit me to offend Thee again. * Grant that I may love Thee always; * and then do with me what Thou wilt. *

(Say) Our Father—Hail Mary—Glory, *or*

Jesus, for Thee I live, * Jesus, for Thee I die. *
Jesus, I am Thine in life and in death. Amen.

Saw her sweet Son, for His na-tion, Saw Him hang in des-o-la-tion Till His Spir-it forth He sent.

Ninth Station

JESUS FALLS THE THIRD TIME.

(Genuflect)

Priest: We adore Thee, O Christ and we bless Thee.

People: Because by Thy Holy Cross Thou hast redeemed the world.

(Stand)

Priest: Consider the third fall of Jesus Christ. His weakness was extreme, and the cruelty of His executioners excessive, who tried to hasten His steps when He had scarcely strength to move.

(Kneel)

People: Ah, my outraged Jesus, * by the merits of the weakness Thou didst suffer in going to Calvary, * give me strength sufficient to conquer all human respect, * and all my wicked passions, * which have led me to despise Thy friendship. * I love Thee, Jesus my Love, with my whole heart; * I repent of having offended Thee. * Never permit me to offend Thee again. * Grant that I may love Thee always, * and then do with me what Thou wilt. *

(Say) Our Father—Hail Mary—Glory, *or*

Jesus, for Thee I live, * Jesus, for Thee I die. * Jesus, I am Thine in life and in death. Amen.

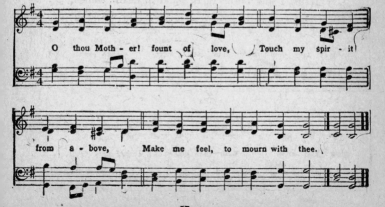

O thou Moth-er! fount of love, Touch my spir-it from a-bove, Make me feel, to mourn with thee.

Tenth Station

JESUS IS STRIPPED OF HIS GARMENTS.

(Genuflect)

Priest: We adore Thee, O Christ and we bless Thee.

People: Because by Thy Holy Cross Thou hast redeemed the world.

(Stand)

Priest: Consider the violence with which the executioners stripped Jesus. His inner garments adhered to His torn flesh, and they dragged them off so roughly that the skin came with them. Compassionate your Savior thus cruelly treated, and say to Him:

(Kneel)

People: My innocent Jesus, * by the merits of the torment Thou hast felt, * help me to strip myself of all affection to things of earth, * in order that I may place all my love in Thee, * who art so worthy of my love. * I love Thee, O Jesus, with my whole heart; * I repent of having offended Thee. * Never permit me to offend Thee again. * Grant that I may love Thee always; * and then do with me what Thou wilt. *

(Say) Our Father—Hail Mary—Glory, *or*

Jesus, for Thee I live, * Jesus, for Thee I die. * Jesus, I am Thine in life and in death. Amen.

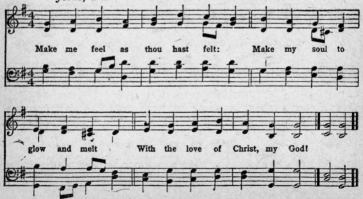

Make me feel as thou hast felt: Make my soul to glow and melt With the love of Christ, my God!

Eleventh Station

JESUS IS NAILED TO THE CROSS.

(Genuflect)

Priest: We adore Thee, O Christ and we bless Thee.

People: Because by Thy Holy Cross Thou hast redeemed the world.

(Stand)

Priest: Consider how Jesus, after having been thrown on the Cross, stretched out His hands, and offered to His Eternal Father the sacrifice of His life for our salvation. These barbarians fastened Him with nails, and then raising the Cross, left Him to die with anguish on this infamous gibbet.

(Kneel)

People: My Jesus, loaded with contempt, * nail my heart to Thy feet, that it may ever remain there, * to love Thee, and never quit Thee again. * I love Thee more than myself; * I repent of having offended Thee. * Never permit me to offend Thee again. * Grant that I may love Thee always, * and then do with me what Thou wilt. *

(Say) Our Father—Hail Mary—Glory, *or*

Jesus, for Thee I live, * Jesus, for Thee I die. *
Jesus, I am Thine in life and in death. Amen.

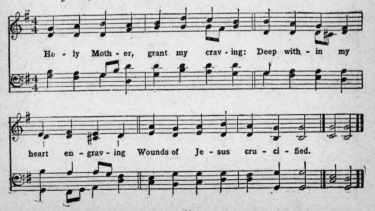

Ho - ly Moth - er, grant my crav - ing: Deep with - in my heart en - grav - ing Wounds of Je - sus cru - ci - fied.

Twelfth Station

JESUS DIES ON THE CROSS.

(Genuflect)

Priest: We adore Thee, O Christ and we bless Thee.

People: Because by Thy Holy Cross Thou hast redeemed the world.

(Stand)

Priest: Consider how Jesus, after three hours' agony on the Cross, consumed at length with anguish, abandons himself to the weight of His body, bows His head, and dies.

(Kneel)

People: O my dying Jesus, * I kiss devoutly the Cross on which Thou didst die for love of me. * I have merited by my sins to die a miserable death; * but Thy death is my hope. * Ah, by the merits of Thy Death, * give me grace to die embracing Thy feet, * and burning with love for Thee. * I yield my soul into Thy hands. * I love Thee with my whole heart; * I repent of ever having offended Thee. * Permit not that I ever offend Thee again. * Grant that I may love Thee always; * and then do with me what Thou wilt. *

(Say) Our Father—Hail Mary—Glory, *or*

Jesus, for Thee I live, * Jesus, for Thee I die. *
Jesus, I am Thine in life and in death. Amen.

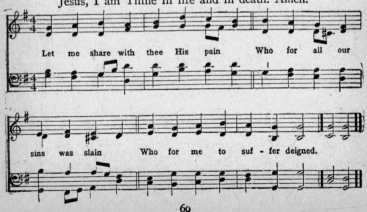

Let me share with thee His pain Who for all our

sins was slain Who for me to suf-fer deigned.

60

Thirteenth Station

JESUS IS TAKEN DOWN FROM THE CROSS.

(Genuflect)

Priest: We adore Thee, O Christ and we bless Thee.

People: Because by Thy Holy Cross Thou hast redeemed the world.

(Stand)

Priest: Consider how our Lord having expired, two of His disciples, Joseph and Nicodemus, took Him down from the Cross, and placed Him in the arms of His afflicted Mother, who received Him with unutterable tenderness and pressed Him to her bosom.

(Kneel)

People: O Mother of sorrow, for the love of this Son, * accept me for Thy servant, and pray to Him for me. * And Thou, my Redeemer, * since Thou hast died for me, * permit me to love Thee; * for I wish but Thee, and nothing more. * I love Thee, my Jesus, * and I repent of ever having offended Thee. * Never permit me to offend Thee again. * Grant that I may love Thee always; * and then do with me what Thou wilt. *

(Say) Our Father—Hail Mary—Glory, *or*

Jesus, for Thee I live, * Jesus, for Thee I die. *
Jesus, I am Thine in life and in death. Amen.

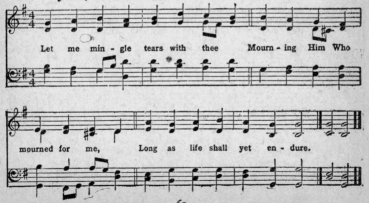

Let me min-gle tears with thee Mourn-ing Him Who mourned for me, Long as life shall yet en-dure.

Fourteenth Station

JESUS IS PLACED IN THE SEPULCHRE.

(Genuflect)

Priest: We adore Thee, O Christ and we bless Thee.

People: Because by Thy Holy Cross Thou hast redeemed the world.

(Stand)

Priest: Consider how the disciples carried the body of Jesus to bury it, accompanied by His holy Mother, who arranged it in the sepulchre with her own hands. They then closed the tomb, and all withdrew.

(Kneel)

People: Ah, my buried Jesus, * I kiss the stone that encloses Thee. * But Thou didst rise again the third day. * I beseech Thee, by Thy resurrection, * make me rise glorious with Thee at the last day, * to be always united with Thee in heaven, * to praise Thee and love Thee forever, * I love Thee, and I repent of ever having offended Thee. * Permit not that I ever offend Thee again. * Grant that I may love Thee; * and then do with me what Thou wilt. *

(Say) Our Father—Hail Mary—Glory, *or*
Jesus, for Thee I live, * Jesus, for Thee I die. *
Jesus, I am Thine in life and in death. Amen.

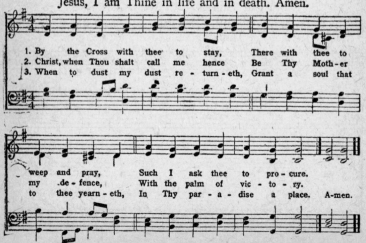

1. By the Cross with thee to stay, There with thee to weep and pray, Such I ask thee to pro-cure.
2. Christ, when Thou shalt call me hence Be Thy Mother my de-fence, With the palm of vic-to-ry.
3. When to dust my dust re-turn-eth, Grant a soul that to thee yearn-eth, In Thy par-a-dise a place. A-men.

Benediction of the Most Blessed Sacrament

Kneeling—All Sing

O Salutaris Hostia

WERNER

1. O sa - lu - tá - ris Hó - sti - a, Quæ cœ - li pan - dis
2. U - ni tri - nó - que Dó - mi - no Sit sem - pi - tér - na

ó - sti - um: Bel - la pre - munt ho - sti - la - a,
gló - ri - a! Qui vi - tam si - ne tér - mi - no,

Da - ro - bur, fer aúx - i - li - um.
No - bis do - net in pá - tri - a. A - men.

Tantum Ergo

WEBBE

1. Tan-tum er - go Sa - cra - mén - tum Ve - ne - ré - mur cér - nu - i,
2. Gen - i - tó - ri, Gen - i - to - que Laus et ju - bi - lá - ti - o,

Tantum Ergo

Et an-ti-quum do-cu-mén-tum No-vo ce-dat-rí-tu-i.
Sa-lus, hon-or, vir-tus quo-que, Sit et be-ne-díc-ti-o.

Prae-stet fi-des supp-le-men-tum, Sén-su-um de-féc-tu-i.
Pro-ce-dén-ti ab u-tro-que, Com-par sit lau-dá-ti-o. A-men.

Priest: Panem de cœlo præstitisti eis; (Alleluia).

People: Omne delectamentum * in se habentem. (Alleluia).

Priest: Oremus: Deus, qui nobis sub Sacramento mirabili passionis tuæ memoriam reliquisti; tribue, quæsumus; ita nos corporis et sanguinis tui sacra mysteria venerari ut redemptionis tuæ fructum in nobis jugiter sentiamus. Qui vivis et regnas in sæcula sæculorum.

People: Amen.

(Repeat aloud after the Priest)

Blessed be God!

Blessed be His Holy Name!

Blessed be Jesus Christ, true God and true Man!

Blessed be the name of Jesus!

Blessed be His most Sacred Heart!

Blessed be Jesus in the most holy Sacrament of the Altar!

Blessed be the great Mother of God, Mary most holy!

Blessed be her holy and Immaculate Conception!

Blessed be the name of Mary, Virgin and Mother.

Blessed be St. Joseph her most chaste Spouse!

Blessed be God in His angels and in His Saints!

To Jesus' Heart All Burning

Rev. A. J. Christie S.J.

Traditional Air

mf

1. To Je - sus' Heart all burn - ing With fer - vent' love for men
2. O Heart for me on fire, With love no man can speak,
3. Too true I have for - sak - en Thy flock by wil - ful sin,
4. As Thou art meek and low - ly, And ev - er pure at Heart,

My heart with fond - est yearn - ing shall raise the joy - ful strain.
My yet un - told de - sire, God gives me for Thy sake.
Yet now let me be tak - en Back to Thy fold a - gain.
So may my heart be whol - ly Of Thine the coun - ter - part.

REFRAIN

f

While a - ges course a - long, Blest be with loud - est song

The Sa - cred Heart of Je - sus By ev' - ry heart and tongue?

The Sa - cred Heart of Je - sus By ev' - ry heart and tongue.

Sacred Heart

Mother Dear, O Pray for Me

Traditional Melody

1. Moth-er dear, O pray for me! Whilst far from heav'n and thee——
2. Moth-er dear, O pray for me! Should pleas-ure's si-ren lay,——
3. Moth-er dear, O pray for me! When all looks bright and fair,

I wan-der in a fra-gile bark O'er life's tem-pes-tuous sea,——
E'er tempt thy child to wan-der far From Vir-tue's path a-way.——
That I may all my dan-ger see, For sure-ly then 'tis near.

O Vir-gin Mother, from thy throne, So bright in bliss a-bove,——
When thorns be-set life's de-vious way, And dark-ling wa-ters flow,——
A moth-er's pray'r how much we need If pros-p'rous be the ray

Pro-tect thy child and cheer my path With thy sweet smile of love.
Then Ma-ry aid thy weep-ing child, Thy-self a moth-er show.
That paints with gold the flow'r-y mead, Which blossoms in our way.

Blessed Virgin

Mother Dear, O Pray for Me

CHORUS

Moth-er dear, re-mem-ber me, And nev-er cease thy care,

Till in heaven e-ter-nal-ly, Thy love and bliss I share.

45   O Lord, I Am Not Worthy

BURNS

1. O Lord, I am not wor-thy   That Thou shouldst come to me,
2. And hum-bly I'll re-ceive Thee,   The Bride-groom of my soul,
3. O Sac-ra-ment most ho-ly!   O Sac-ra-ment di-vine!

But speak the words of com-fort,   My spir-it healed shall be.
No more by sin to grieve Thee,   Or fly Thy sweet con-trol.
All praise and all thanks-giv-ing   Be ev-ery mo-ment Thine.

Blessed Sacrament

Reprinted from The American Catholic Hymnal. Copyright by P. J. Kenedy & Sons, New York.

Holy God, We Praise Thy Name

REV. C. WALWORTH   P. RITTER

1. Ho - ly God, we praise Thy Name! Lord of all, we
2. Hark! the loud ce - les - tial hymn, An - gel choirs a -
3. Lo! the a - pos - tol - ic train Join Thy sa - cred
4. Ho - ly Fa - ther, Ho - ly Son, Ho - ly Spir - it,
5. Thou art King of Glo - ry Christ! Son of God, yet

bow be - fore Thee! All on earth Thy scep - tre claim,
bove are rais - ing! Che - ru - bim and Se - ra - phim,
Name to hal - low! Prophets swell the loud re - frain,
Three we name Thee, While in es - sence on - ly One,
born of Ma - ry, For us sin - ners sac - ri - ficed,

REFRAIN

All in heav'n a - bove a - dore Thee: In - fi - nite Thy
In un - ceas - ing chor - us prais - ing; Fill the Heav'ns with
And with white - robed mar - tyrs fol - low; And from morn till
Un - di - vid - ed God we claim Thee: And a - dor - ing
And to death a - trib - u - ta - ry: First to break the

vast do - main, Ev - er - last - ing is Thy Reign.
sweet ac - cord; Ho - ly! Ho - ly! Ho - ly Lord.
set of sun, Through the Church the song goes on.
bend the knee, While we own the mys - te - ry.
bars of death, Thou hast o - pen'd heav'n to Faith.

God
Reprinted from The American Catholic Hymnal. Copyright by P. J. Kenedy & Sons, New York.

47   Order for Jewish Service

People:

O my God, the soul which Thou gavest me is pure; Thou didst create it, Thou didst form it, Thou didst breathe it into me; Thou preservest it within me; and Thou wilt take it from me, but wilt restore it unto me hereafter. So long as the soul is within me, I will give thanks unto Thee, O Lord my God and God of my fathers, Sovereign of all works, Lord of all souls!

Chaplain:

Bless ye the Lord who is to be blessed.
Blessed is the Lord who is to be blessed for ever and ever.

People:

All Singing:

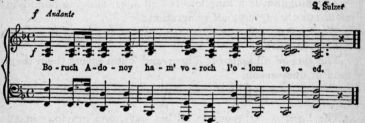

Bo-ruch A-do-noy ha-m' vo-roch l'o-lom vo-ed.

Responsive Reading:

Happy are they that dwell in thy House: they will be ever praising Thee.

Happy is the people, that is in such a case, yea, happy is the people, whose God is the Lord.

I will extol Thee, my God, O King; and I will bless Thy name for ever and ever.

Every day will I bless Thee; and I will praise Thy name for ever and ever.

Great is the Lord, and highly to be praised; and his greatness is unsearchable.

One generation shall laud thy works to another, and shall declare thy mighty acts.

The glorious splendour of thy majesty, and thy wondrous works, will I rehearse.

And men shall speak of the might of thy tremendous acts; and I will tell of thy greatness.

They shall utter the fame of thy great goodness, and shall sing of thy righteousness.

The Lord is gracious and full of compassion; slow to anger and of great mercy.

The Lord is good to all; and his tender mercies are over all his works.

All thy works shall praise Thee, O Lord; and thy saints shall bless Thee.

They shall speak of the glory of thy kingdom, and talk of thy might; to make known to the sons of men his mighty acts, and the glory of the majesty of his kingdom.

Thy kingdom is a kingdom for all ages, and thy dominion endureth throughout all generations.

The Lord upholdeth all that fall, and raiseth up all those that are bowed down.

The eyes of all wait for Thee; and Thou givest them their food in due season.

Thou openest thy hand, and satisfiest every living thing with favour.

The Lord is righteous in all his ways, and gracious in all his works.

The Lord is nigh unto all them that call upon Him, to all that call upon Him in truth.

He will fulfil the desire of them that fear Him; He also will hear their cry, and will save them.

The Lord preserveth all them that love Him; but all the wicked will He destroy.

My mouth shall speak the praise of the Lord; and let all flesh bless his holy name for ever and ever.

Chaplain:

Hear, O Israel: The Lord our God, the Lord is One.
Sh'ma Yis-ro-ayl A-do-noy E-lo-hay-nu, A-do-noy e-chod.

People:

All Singing:

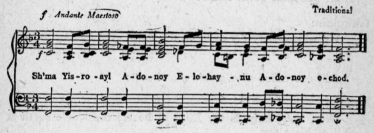

f *Andante Maestoso*

Traditional

Sh'ma Yis-ro-ayl A-do-noy E-lo-hay-nu A-do-noy e-chod.

People:

And thou shalt love the Lord thy God with all thy heart, and
with all thy soul, and with all thy might. And these words, which
I command thee this day, shall be upon thy heart; and thou shalt
teach them diligently unto thy children, and shalt talk of them
when thou sittest in thy house, and when thou walkest by the
way, and when thou liest down, and when thou risest up. And
thou shalt bind them for a sign upon thy hand, and they shall
be for frontlets between thine eyes. And thou shalt write them
upon the doorposts of thy house, and upon thy gates.

Responsive Reading:

A Song of Ascents

I will lift up mine eyes unto the mountains: From whence
shall my help come?

My help cometh from the Lord, who made heaven and
earth.

He will not suffer thy foot to be moved; he that keepeth thee
will not slumber.

Behold, He that keepeth Israel doth neither slumber nor sleep.

The Lord is thy keeper; the Lord is thy shade upon thy right hand.

The sun shall not smite thee by day, nor the moon by night.

The Lord shall keep thee from all evil; He shall keep thy soul.

The Lord shall guard thy going out and thy coming in, from this time forth and for ever.

Chaplain:

We will sanctify thy name in the world even as they sanctify it in the highest heavens, as it is written by the hand of thy prophet:

And one called unto another, and said:

People:

Holy, holy, holy, is the Lord of hosts; the whole earth is full of his glory.

People:

Kodosh

S. Sulzer

Ko - dosh, ko - dosh, ko - dosh A - do - noy ts'vo -

os   m'lo chol ho - o - rets k'vo - do.

os   m' - lo chol —— ho - o - rets

Chaplain:

Blessed is the Lord who is to be blessed for ever and ever.

People:

Boruch K'vod

S. Sulzer

Bo - ruch k - vod A - do - noy mi - m' - ko - mo.

Chaplain:

The Lord shall reign for ever, thy God, O Zion, unto all generations. Halleluyah!

People:

Yimloch

S. Sulzer

Yim - loch A - do - noy l'o - lom E - lo - ha - yich Tsee

yon, l'dor vo - dor, Hal - l' - lu - yo.
l'-dor vo - dor l'dor vo-dor Hal - l' - lu - yo

l' - dor vo - dor

73

Sermon

People:

En Kelohenu
(THERE IS NONE LIKE GOD)

1. En ke lo he nu, En ka do ne nu, En k' mal ke nu En k'mo shi e nu. 2. Mi che lo he nu,

3. No de le lo he hu, No de la do ne nu, No de l' mal ke nu, No de l'mo shi e nu. 4. Bo ruch e lo he nu,

Mi cha do ne nu, Mi ch' mal ke nu, Mi ch' mo shi e nu.

Bo ruch a do ne nu, Bo ruch mal ke nu, Bo ruch mo shi e nu.

5. At to hu e lo he nu, At to hu a do ne nu,

At to hu mal ke nu, At to hu mo shi e nu.

74

Chaplain:

Let the words of my mouth and the meditation of my heart be acceptable before Thee, O Lord, my Rock and my Redeemer. He who maketh peace in His high places, may He make peace for us and for all Israel, and say ye: "Amen."

People:

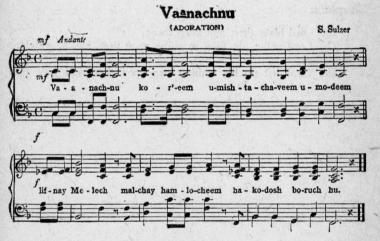

Vaanachnu

(ADORATION)

S. Sulzer

Va - a - nach-nu   ko - r'-eem   u-mish - ta - cha-veem u - mo-deem

lif-nay Me - lech   mal-chay ham - lo-cheem   ha - ko-dosh   bo-ruch hu.

For we bend the knee and offer worship and thanks before The Supreme King of Kings, the Holy One, blessed be He.

Kaddish

Mourners:

Yis'gadal v'yis'kadash sh'mey rabbo. B'ol'mo dee-v'ro chir'usey v'yam'lich mal'chusey, b'chayeichon uv'yomeichon uv'chayey d'chol beis yis'roeil, ba'agolo uviz'man koreev v'im'roo omein. Y'hey sh'mey rabbo m'vorach l'olam ul'olmey ol'mayoh. Yis'borach v'yish'tabach v'yis'poar v'yis'roman v'yis'nassey, v'yis'hadar v'yis'alleh v'yis'hallal sh'mey d'kud'sho b'rich hoo. L'eylo min

kol bir'choso v'sheeroso tush'b'choso v'nech'moso da'ameeron
b'ol'mo v'im'roo omein. Y'hey sh'lomo rabbo min sh'mayo
v'chayim oleinoo v'al kol yis'roeil v'im'roo omein. Oseh sholom
bim'romov hoo ya'aseh sholom oleinoo v'al kol yis'roeil v'im'roo
omein.

Benediction

Chaplain:

The Lord bless thee, and keep thee;
The Lord make his face to shine upon thee, and be gracious
unto thee;
The Lord lift up his countenance upon thee, and give thee
peace.

The music in the Jewish Section is presented by the Central Conference of
American Rabbis.

48   Rejoice, ye Pure in Heart

Marion S. M. With Refrain

Edward H. Plumptre, 1865   Arthur H. Messiter, 1883

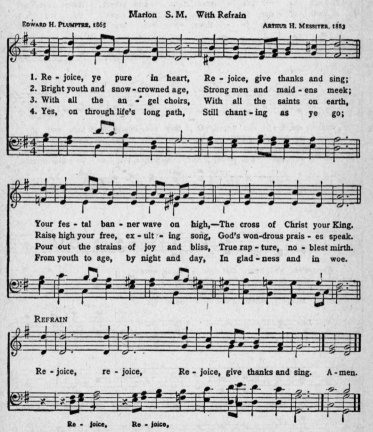

1. Re - joice, ye pure in heart, Re - joice, give thanks and sing;
2. Bright youth and snow - crowned age, Strong men and maid - ens meek;
3. With all the an - gel choirs, With all the saints on earth,
4. Yes, on through life's long path, Still chant - ing as ye go;

Your fes - tal ban - ner wave on high,—The cross of Christ your King.
Raise high your free, ex - ult - ing song, God's won - drous prais - es speak.
Pour out the strains of joy and bliss, True rap - ture, no - blest mirth.
From youth to age, by night and day, In glad - ness and in woe.

REFRAIN

Re - joice, re - joice, Re - joice, give thanks and sing. A - men.

Re - joice, Re - joice,

Faith of our Fathers, Living Still

St. Catherine L. M. With Refrain

FREDERICK W. FABER 1849

HENRY F. HEMY and J. G. WALTON, 1874

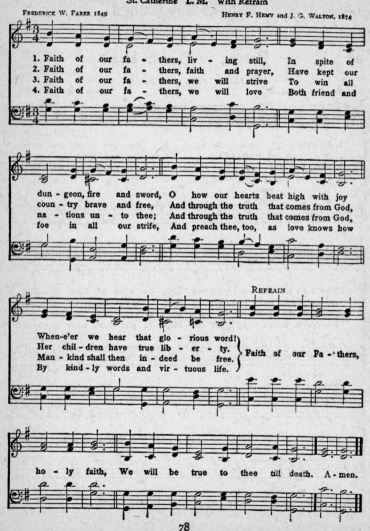

1. Faith of our fa - thers, liv - ing still, In spite of dun - geon, fire and sword, O how our hearts beat high with joy When-e'er we hear that glo - rious word!
2. Faith of our fa - thers, faith and prayer, Have kept our coun - try brave and free, And through the truth that comes from God, Her chil - dren have true lib - er - ty.
3. Faith of our fa - thers, we will strive To win all na - tions un - to thee; And through the truth that comes from God, Man - kind shall then in - deed be free.
4. Faith of our fa - thers, we will love Both friend and foe in all our strife, And preach thee, too, as love knows how By kind - ly words and vir - tuous life.

REFRAIN

Faith of our Fa - thers, ho - ly faith, We will be true to thee till death. A - men.

Holy, Holy, Holy, Lord God Almighty

Nicaea 11 12 12 10

REGINALD HEBER, 1826

JOHN B. DYKES, 1861

1. Ho - ly, ho - ly, ho - ly! Lord God Al - might - y!
2. Ho - ly, ho - ly, ho - ly! all the saints a - dore Thee,
3. Ho - ly, ho - ly, ho - ly! tho' the dark - ness hide Thee,
4. Ho - ly, ho - ly, ho - ly! Lord God Al - might - y!

Ear - ly in the morn - ing our song shall rise to Thee;
Cast - ing down their gold - en crowns a - round the glass - y sea;
Though the eye of sin - ful man Thy glo - ry may not see,
All Thy works shall praise Thy name, in earth, and sky, and sea;

Ho - ly, ho - ly, ho - ly, mer - ci - ful and might - y!
Cher - u - bim and sera - phim fall - ing down be - fore Thee,
On - ly Thou art ho - ly, there is none be - side Thee,
Ho - ly, ho - ly, ho - ly, mer - ci - ful and might - y!

God in three per - sons, bless - ed Trin - i - ty!
Which wert, and art, and ev - er - more shalt be.
Per - fect in power, in love, and pu - ri - ty.
God in three per - sons, bless - ed Trin - i - ty! A - men.

51 Day is Dying in the West

Chautauqua 77774 With Refrain

MARY A. LATHBURY, 1877   WILLIAM F. SHERWIN, 1877

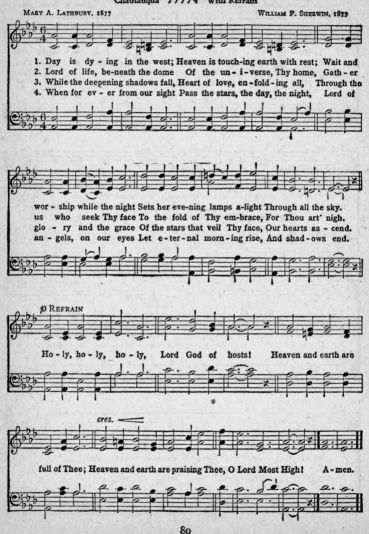

1. Day is dy-ing in the west; Heaven is touch-ing earth with rest; Wait and wor-ship while the night Sets her eve-ning lamps a-light Through all the sky.

2. Lord of life, be-neath the dome Of the un-i-verse, Thy home, Gath-er us who seek Thy face To the fold of Thy em-brace, For Thou art' nigh.

3. While the deepening shadows fall, Heart of love, en-fold-ing all, Through the glo-ry and the grace Of the stars that veil Thy face, Our hearts as-cend.

4. When for ev-er from our sight Pass the stars, the day, the night, Lord of an-gels, on our eyes Let e-ter-nal morn-ing rise, And shad-ows end.

Refrain

Ho-ly, ho-ly, ho-ly, Lord God of hosts! Heaven and earth are full of Thee; Heaven and earth are praising Thee, O Lord Most High! A-men.

52   Joy to the World! The Lord is Come

Antioch C. M.

Isaac Watts, 1719

Arr. fr. G. F. Handel, 1742, by Lowell Mason, 1836

1. Joy to the world! the Lord is come;   Let earth re - ceive her King;
2. Joy to the earth; the Sav - iour reigns;   Let men their songs em - ploy;
3. No more let sins and sor - rows grow,   Nor thorns in - fest the ground,
4. He rules the world with truth and grace,   And makes the na - tions prove

Let   eve - ry   heart   pre - pare   Him   room,
While fields   and   floods,   rocks,   hills,   and   plains,
He   comes   to   make   His   bless - ings   flow
The   glo - ries   of   His   right - eous - ness,

And heaven and na - ture sing,   And heaven and na - ture sing,
Re - peat the sound - ing joy,   Re - peat the sound-ing joy,
Far   as the curse is found,   Far   as the curse is found,
And   won - ders of His love,   And   won - ders of His love,

And   heaven   and na - ture   sing,

And   heaven and na - ture   sing,   And   heaven and na -

And   heaven,   and   heaven   and na - ture   sing.
Re - peat,   re - peat   the sound - ing   joy.
Far   as,   far   as   the curse is   found.
And   won - ders, won - ders of His   love.   A - men.

ture   sing,

Hark! the Herald Angels Sing

Mendelssohn 7 7 7 7 D

CHARLES WESLEY, 1739; altered by GEORGE WHITFIELD, 1753

Arr. from MENDELSSOHN, 1840
by WILLIAM CUMMINGS, 1850

1. Hark! the her-ald an-gels sing, "Glo-ry to the new-born King;
2. Christ, by high-est heaven a-dored; Christ, the ev-er-last-ing Lord!
3. Hail, the heaven-born Prince of Peace! Hail, the Sun of Right-eous-ness!

Peace on earth, and mer-cy mild, God and sin-ners rec-on-ciled!"
Come, De-sire of Na-tions, come, Fix in us Thy hum-ble home.
Light and life to all He brings, Ris'n with heal-ing in His wings.

Joy-ful all ye na-tions, rise, Join the tri-umph of the skies;
Veiled in flesh the God-head see; Hail th'In-car-nate De-i-ty,
Mild He lays His glo-ry by, Born that man no more may die,

With th'an-gel-ic host pro-claim "Christ is born in Beth-le-hem."
Pleased as man with man to dwell; Je-sus, our Em-man-u-el.
Born to raise the sons of earth, Born to give them sec-ond birth.

Hark! the her-ald an-gels sing, "Glo-ry to the new-born King." A-men.

Ped.

54   O Little Town of Bethlehem

St. Louis 86867686

PHILLIPS BROOKS, 1868   LEWIS H. REDNER, 1868

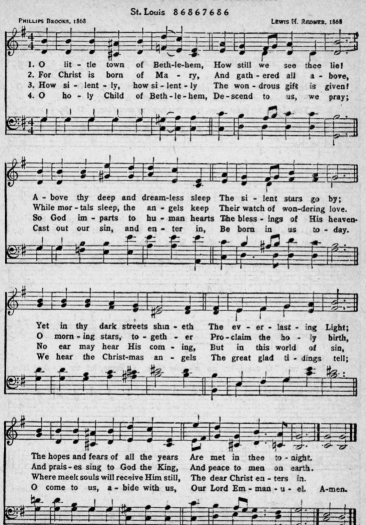

1. O lit-tle town of Beth-le-hem, How still we see thee lie!
2. For Christ is born of Ma - ry, And gath-ered all a - bove,
3. How si - lent-ly, how si-lent-ly The won-drous gift is given!
4. O ho - ly Child of Beth-le-hem, De-scend to us, we pray;

A - bove thy deep and dream-less sleep The si - lent stars go by;
While mor - tals sleep, the an-gels keep Their watch of won-dering love.
So God im - parts to hu - man hearts The bless - ings of His heaven-
Cast out our sin, and en - ter in, Be born in us to - day.

Yet in thy dark streets shin - eth The ev-er-last-ing Light;
O morn - ing stars, to-geth - er Pro-claim the ho - ly birth,
No ear may hear His com - ing, But in this world of sin,
We hear the Christ-mas an - gels The great glad ti - dings tell;

The hopes and fears of all the years Are met in thee to - night.
And prais - es sing to God the King, And peace to men on earth.
Where meek souls will receive Him still, The dear Christ en - ters in.
O come to us, a - bide with us, Our Lord Em - man - u - el. A-men.

O Come, All Ye Faithful

Adeste Fideles   Irregular

Latin Hymn, 17th Century
Tr. Frederick Oakeley, 1841

Anonymous in
Wade's Cantus Diversi, 1751

1. O come, all ye faith-ful, joy-ful and tri-umph-ant, O come ye, O
come ye to Beth - le - hem; Come and be-hold Him born the King of
an - gels;   O come, let us a-dore Him, O come, let us a-dore Him,
O come, let us a-dore Him, Christ, the Lord.   A-men.

2. Sing, choirs of an - gels, sing in ex - ul - ta - tion, O sing, all ye
cit-i-zens of heaven a - bove; Glo - ry to God, all glo - ry in the
high - est;

3. Yea, Lord, we greet Thee, born this hap - py morn-ing, O Je - sus, to
Thee be all glo - ry given; Word of the Fa - ther, now in flesh ap-
pear - ing;

Silent Night, Holy Night

Silent Night   Irregular

Joseph Mohr, 1818   Franz Gruber, 1818

1. Si - lent night, ho - ly night, All is calm, all is bright
2. Si - lent night, ho - ly night, Dark - ness flies, and all is light;
3. Si - lent night, ho - ly night, Guid - ing Star, O lend thy light;
4. Si - lent night, ho - ly night, Won - drous Star, O lend thy light;

Round yon Vir - gin Moth - er and Child, Ho - ly In - fant so
Shep - herds hear the an - gels sing, "Al - le - lu - ia!
See the east - ern wise men bring Gifts and hom - age
With the an - gels let us sing Al - le - lu - ia

ten - der and mild, Sleep in heav - en - ly
hail the King! Je - sus the Sav - iour is
to our King; Je - sus the Sav - iour is
to our King! Je - sus our Sav - iour is

peace   Sleep in heav - en - ly peace.
here, Je - sus the Sav - iour is here."
here, Je - sus the Sav - iour is here.
here, Je - sus our Sav - iour is here.   A - men.

Good King Wenceslas

John Neal

Traditional

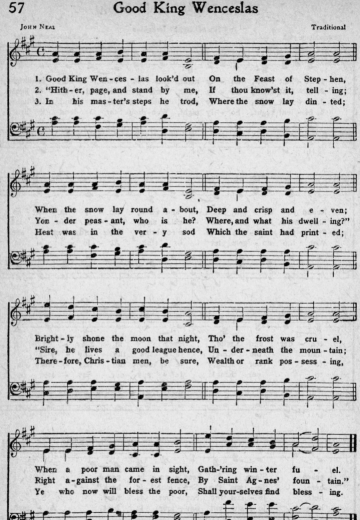

1. Good King Wen-ces-las look'd out On the Feast of Step-hen,
2. "Hith-er, page, and stand by me, If thou know'st it, tell-ing;
3. In his mas-ter's steps he trod, Where the snow lay din-ted;

When the snow lay round a-bout, Deep and crisp and e-ven;
Yon-der peas-ant, who is he? Where, and what his dwell-ing?"
Heat was in the ver-y sod Which the saint had print-ed;

Bright-ly shone the moon that night, Tho' the frost was cru-el,
"Sire, he lives a good league hence, Un-der-neath the moun-tain;
There-fore, Chris-tian men, be sure, Wealth or rank pos-sess-ing,

When a poor man came in sight, Gath-'ring win-ter fu-el.
Right a-gainst the for-est fence, By Saint Ag-nes' foun-tain."
Ye who now will bless the poor, Shall your-selves find bless-ing.

58 In the Lonely Midnight

Lonely Midnight 6 5 6 5 D

THEODORE CHICKERING WILLIAMS

ALONZO POTTER HOWARD

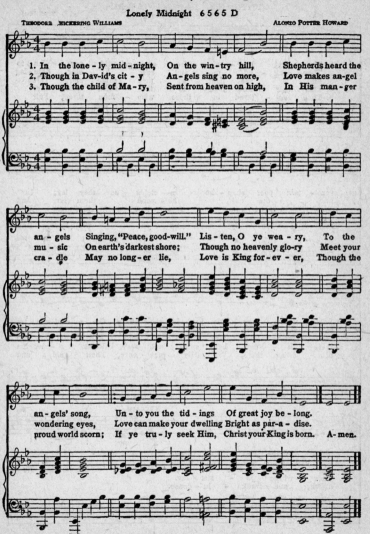

1. In the lone-ly mid-night, On the win-try hill, Shepherds heard the
2. Though in Dav-id's cit-y An-gels sing no more, Love makes an-gel
3. Though the child of Ma-ry, Sent from heaven on high, In His man-ger

an-gels Singing, "Peace, good-will." Lis-ten, O ye wea-ry, To the
mu-sic On earth's darkest shore; Though no heavenly glo-ry Meet your
cra-dle May no long-er lie, Love is King for-ev-er, Though the

an-gels' song, Un-to you the tid-ings Of great joy be-long.
wondering eyes, Love can make your dwelling Bright as par-a-dise.
proud world scorn; If ye tru-ly seek Him, Christ your King is born. A-men.

The First Noel the Angel did Say

The First Noel   Irregular   With Refrain

Traditional   Traditional

1. The first No - el the an - gel did say Was to
2. They look - ed up and saw a star Shin - ing
3. And by the light of that same star, Three
4. This star drew nigh to the north - west, O'er
5. Then en - tered in those wise - men three, Full

cer - tain poor shep - herds in fields as they lay; In
in the east, be - yond them far, And
wise - men came from coun - try far; To
Beth - le - hem it took its rest, And
rev - er - ent - ly up - on the knee, And

fields where they lay keep - ing their sheep, On a cold win - ter's
to the earth it gave great light, And so it con -
seek for a king was their in - tent, And to fol - low the
there it did both stop and stay, Right o - ver the
of - fered there, in His pres - ence, Their gold, and

REFRAIN

night that was so deep.
tin - ued both day and night.
star wher - ev - er it went.   No - el, No - el, No -
place where Je - sus lay.
myrrh, and frank - in - cense.

The First Noel the Angel did Say

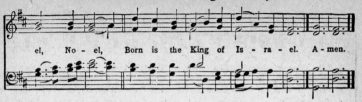

el, No - el, Born is the King of Is - ra - el. A - men.

60 · All Hail the Power of Jesus' Name
Coronation C. M.

EDWARD PERRONET, 1779
Vs. 4 and 5 by JOHN RIPPON, 1787

OLIVER HOLDEN, 1793

1. All hail the power of Je - sus' name! Let an - gels pros - trate fall;
2. Ye seed of Is - rael's cho - sen race, Ye ran - somed of the fall;
3. Sin - ners, whose love can ne'er for - get The worm-wood and the gall,
4. Let eve - ry kin - dred, eve - ry tribe, On this ter - res - trial ball,
5. O that with yon - der sa - cred throng, We at His feet may fall;

Bring forth the roy - al di - a - dem, And crown Him Lord of all,
Hail Him, who saves you by His grace, And crown Him Lord of all,
Go, spread your tro - phies at His feet, And crown Him Lord of all,
To Him all maj - es - ty as - cribe, And crown Him Lord of all,
We'll join the ev - er - last - ing song, And crown Him Lord of all,

Bring forth the roy - al di - a - dem, And crown Him Lord of all.
Hail Him, who saves you by His grace, And crown Him Lord of all.
Go, spread your trophies at His feet, And crown Him Lord of all.
To Him all maj - es - ty as - cribe, And crown Him Lord of all.
We'll join the ev - er - last - ing song, And crown Him Lord of all.

Angels We Have Heard on High

Bishop Chadwick

Old French Melody

1. An - gels we have heard on high, Sweet - ly sing - ing o'er the plains,
2. Shepherds, why this ju - bi - lee? Why your joy - ous strains pro-long?
3. Come to Beth - le - hem, come and see, Him whose birth the an - gels sing;
4. See with - in a man - ger laid, Je - sus, Lord of heaven and earth!

And the moun - tains in re - ply Ech - o back their joy - ous strains.
Say what may the ti - dings be, Which in-spire your heav'n - ly song.
Come a - dore on bend - ed knee, The Infant Christ, the new - born King.
Ma - ry, Jo - seph, lend your aid, With us sing our Sav - iour's birth.

Glo - - - - - - ri - a in ex - cel - sis De - o

Glo - - - - - - ri - a in ex - cel - sis De - o.

Christ the Lord is Risen Today

Worgan 7777 With Alleluia

CHARLES WESLEY, 1739

Arr. from *Lyra Davidica*, 1708

1. "Christ the Lord is risen to - day," Al - le - lu - ia!
2. Lives a - gain our glo - rious King; Al - le - lu - ia!
3. Love's re - deem - ing work is done, Al - le - lu - ia!
4. Soar we now, where Christ has led, Al - le - lu - ia!

Sons of men and an - gels say; Al - le - lu - ia!
Where, O death, is now thy sting? Al - le - lu - ia!
Fought the fight, the bat - tle won; Al - le - lu - ia!
Follow-ing our ex - alt - ed Head; Al - le - lu - ia!

Raise your joys and tri - umphs high, Al - le - lu - ia!
Dy - ing once, He all doth save; Al - le - lu - ia!
Death in vain for - bids Him rise; Al - le - lu - ia!
Made like Him, like Him we rise; Al - le - lu - ia!

Sing, ye heavens and earth re - ply. Al - le - lu - ia!
Where thy vic - to - ry, O grave? Al - le - lu - ia!
Christ has o - pened Par - a - dise. Al - le - lu - ia!
Ours the cross, the grave, the skies. Al - le - lu - ia! A-men.

Beneath the Cross of Jesus

St. Christopher 7 6 8 6 8 6 8 6

Elizabeth C. Clephane, 1868

Frederick C. Maker, 1881

1. Be - neath the cross of Je - sus I fain would take my stand,
2. Up - on that cross of Je - sus Mine eye at times can see
3. I take, O cross, thy shad - ow For my a - bid - ing place;

The shad - ow of a might - y rock With - in a wea - ry land;
The ver - y dy - ing form of One Who suf - fered there for me;
I ask no oth - er sun - shine than The sun - shine of His face;

A home with - in the wil - der - ness, A rest up - on the way,
And from my smit - ten heart with tears Two won - ders I con - fess,—
Con - tent to let the world go by, To know no gain nor loss,

From the burn - ing of the noon - tide heat, And the bur - den of the day.
The won - ders of His glo - rious love And my un - wor - thi - ness.
My sin - ful self my on - ly shame, My glo - ry all the cross. A - men.

64 My Jesus, I Love Thee

Gordon 11 11 11 11

Anonymous

ADONIRAM J. GORDON, 1836-1895

1. My Je - sus, I love Thee, I know Thou art mine,
2. I love Thee, be - cause Thou hast first lov - ed me,
3. I will love Thee in life, I will love Thee in death,
4. In man - sions of glo - ry and end - less de - light,

For Thee all the fol - lies of sin I re - sign;
And pur - chased my par - don on Cal - va - ry's tree;
And praise Thee as long as Thou lend - est me breath;
I'll ev - er a - dore Thee in heav - en so bright;

My gra - cious Re - deem - er, my Sav - iour art Thou;
I love Thee for wear - ing the thorns on Thy brow;
And say when the death - dew lies cold on my brow,
I'll sing with the glit - ter - ing crown on my brow,

If ev - er I loved Thee, my Je - sus 'tis now. A-men.

Tell Me the Old, Old Story

EVANGEL, 7.6.7.6. D. With Refrain

KATHERINE HANKEY, 1834-1911

WILLIAM H. DOANE, 1832-1915

1. Tell me the old, old sto - ry, Of un-seen things a - bove, Of Je - sus
2. Tell me the sto - ry slow - ly, That I may take it in— That won-der
3. Tell me the sto - ry soft - ly, With earn-est tones, and grave; Re - mem-ber!
4. Tell me the same old sto - ry, When you have cause to fear That this world's

and His glo - ry, Of Je - sus and His love. Tell me the sto-ry sim - ply, As
ful re - demp-tion, God's rem-e-dy for sin. Tell me the sto-ry oft - en, For
I'm the sin - ner Whom Je-sus came to save; Tell me that sto-ry al - ways, If
emp - ty glo - ry Is cost-ing me too dear. Yes, and when that world's glory Is

to a lit - tle child, For I am weak and wea-ry, And help-less and de - filed.
I for-get so soon, The "ear-ly dew" of morn-ing Has pass'd a-way at noon.
you would really be, In a - ny time of trou-ble, A com-fort-er to me.
dawning on my soul, Tell me the old, old sto-ry: "Christ Jesus makes thee whole."

REFRAIN

Tell me the old, old sto - ry, Tell me the old, old sto - ry,

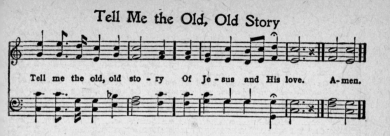

Tell Me the Old, Old Story

Tell me the old, old sto-ry Of Je-sus and His love. A-men.

66

Must Jesus Bear the Cross Alone

Maitland C. M.

REV. THOMAS SHEPHERD, 1692: alt.

GEORGE N ALLEN, 1812-1877

1. Must Je - sus bear the cross a - lone, And
2. How hap - py are the saints a - bove, Who
3. The con - se - crat - ed cross I'll bear, Till
4. Up - on the crys - tal pave - ment, down At
5. O pre - cious cross! O glo - rious crown! O

all the world go free? No, there's a cross for
once went sor - 'wing here; But now they taste un -
death shall set me free; And then go home my
Je - sus' pierc - èd feet, Joy - ful, I'll cast my
res - ur - rec - tion day! Ye an - gels, from the

ev - 'ry one, And there's a cross for me.
ming - led love, And joy with - out a tear.
crown to wear, For there's a crown for me.
gold - en crown, And His dear name re - peat.
stars come down, And bear my soul a - way. A-men.

67 The Old Rugged Cross

George Bennard

George Bennard

1. On a hill far a-way stood an old rug-ged cross, The em-blem of
2. Oh, that old rug-ged cross, so de-spised by the world, Has a won-drous at-
3. In the old rug-ged cross, stained with blood so di-vine, A won-drous
4. To the old rug-ged cross I will ev-er be true, Its shame and re-

suf-fering and shame; And I love that old cross where the dear-est and best
trac-tion for me; For the dear Lamb of God left His glo-ry a-bove
beau-ty I see; For 'twas on that old cross Je-sus suf-fered and died
proach glad-ly bear; Then He'll call me some day to my home far a-way,

Chorus

For a world of lost sin-ners was slain.
To bear it to dark Cal-va-ry. So I'll cher-ish the old rug-ged
To par-don and sanc-ti-fy me.
Where His glo-ry for-ev-er I'll share.

cross, Till my tro-phies at last I lay down; I will cling to the
old rug-ged cross,

old rug-ged cross, And ex-change it some day for a crown.
cross, the old rug-ged cross,

Copyright, 1941, Renewal. The Rodeheaver Co. Owner, Used by permission.

Take My Life, and Let It Be

Hendon 7777

Frances R. Havergal, 1874

Henri A. C. Malan, 1827

1. Take my life, and let it be Con-se-cra-ted, Lord, to thee; Take my hands, and
2. Take my voice, and let me sing, Al-ways, on-ly, for my King. Take my lips, and
3. Take my will, and make it thine; It shall be no longer mine. Take my heart, it
4. Take my love; my Lord, I pour At thy feet its treasure-store. Take my-self, and

let them move At the im-pulse of thy love, At the im-pulse of thy love.
let them be Filled with messa-ges from thee, Filled with messages from thee.
is thine own; It shall be thy roy-al throne, It shall be thy roy-al throne.
I will be Ev-er, on-ly, all for thee, Ev-er, on-ly, all for thee. A-men.

Jesus, the Very Thought of Thee

St. Agnes C. M.

Anonymous Latin hymn, 11th century
Translated by Edward Caswall, 1849

John B. Dykes, 1866

1. Je-sus, the ver-y thought of Thee, With sweetness fills my breast;
2. Nor voice can sing, nor heart can frame, Nor can the mem-ory find
3. O Hope of ev-ery con-trite heart, O Joy of all the meek,
4. Je-sus, our on-ly joy be Thou, As Thou our prize wilt be;

But sweeter far Thy face to see, And in Thy pres-ence rest.
A sweeter sound than Thy blest name, O Sav-iour of man-kind.
To those who fall, how kind Thou art! How good to those who seek!
Je-sus, be Thou our glo-ry now, And through e-ter-ni-ty. A-men.

He Leadeth Me

He Leadeth Me L. M. With Refrain

JOSEPH H. GILMORE, 1862

WILLIAM B. BRADBURY, 1854

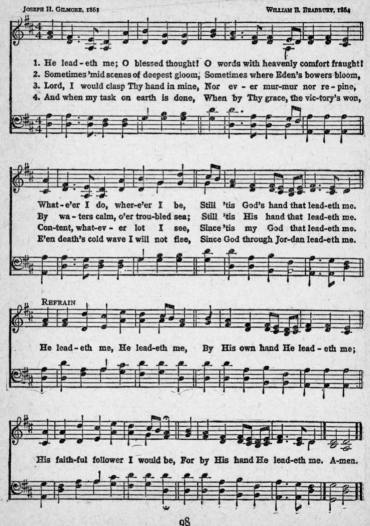

1. He lead-eth me; O blessed thought! O words with heavenly comfort fraught!
2. Sometimes 'mid scenes of deepest gloom, Sometimes where Eden's bowers bloom,
3. Lord, I would clasp Thy hand in mine, Nor ev-er mur-mur nor re-pine,
4. And when my task on earth is done, When by Thy grace, the vic-tory's won,

What-e'er I do, wher-e'er I be, Still 'tis God's hand that lead-eth me:
By wa-ters calm, o'er trou-bled sea; Still 'tis His hand that lead-eth me.
Con-tent, what-ev-er lot I see, Since 'tis my God that lead-eth me.
E'en death's cold wave I will not flee, Since God through Jor-dan lead-eth me.

REFRAIN

He lead-eth me, He lead-eth me, By His own hand He lead-eth me;

His faith-ful follower I would be, For by His hand He lead-eth me. A-men.

Saviour, Like a Shepherd

Bradbury 873747

In *Hymns for the Young,* 1836   WILLIAM B. BRADBURY, 1859

1. Sav - iour, like a shep-herd lead us,   Much we need Thy ten-der care;
2. We are Thine; do Thou be - friend us,   Be the guar-dian of our way;
3. Thou hast prom-ised to re - ceive us,   Poor and sin-ful though we be;
4. Ear - ly let us seek Thy fa - vor,   Ear - ly let us do Thy will;

In Thy pleas-ant pas-tures feed us;   For our use Thy folds pre-pare.
Keep Thy flock, from sin de - fend us;   Seek us when we go a - stray.
Thou hast mer-cy to re - lieve us,   Grace to cleanse, and power to free.
Bless-ed Lord and on - ly Sav - iour,   With Thy love our bos-oms ill.

Bless-ed Je - sus, Bless-ed Je - sus, Thou hast bought us, Thine we are;
Bless-ed Je - sus, Bless-ed Je - sus, Hear the chil-dren, when they pray;
Bless-ed Je - sus, Bless-ed Je - sus, Ear - ly let us turn to Thee;
Bless-ed Je - sus, Bless-ed Je - sus, Thou hast loved us, love us still;

Bless-ed Je-sus, Bless-ed Je-sus, Thou hast bought us, Thine we are.
Bless-ed Je-sus, Bless-ed Je-sus, Hear the chil-dren, when they pray.
Bless-ed Je-sus, Bless-ed Je-sus, Ear - ly let us turn to Thee.
Bless-ed Je-sus, Bless-ed Je-sus, Thou hast loved us, love us still. A-men.

I Love to Tell the Story

Hankey 7676 D With Refrain

KATHERINE HANKEY, 1870

WILLIAM G. FISCHER, 1869

1. I love to tell the story Of un-seen things a-bove,
2. I love to tell the story; 'Tis pleas-ant to re-peat
3. I love to tell the story; For those who know it best

Of Je-sus and His glo-ry, Of Je-sus and His love.
What seems, each time I tell it, More won-der-ful-ly sweet.
Seem hun-ger-ing and thirst-ing To hear it, like the rest.

I love to tell the story, Be-cause I know 'tis true,
I love to tell the story, For some have nev-er heard
And when, in scenes of glo-ry, I sing the new, new song,

It sat-is-fies my long-ings As noth-ing else could do.
The mes-sage of sal-va-tion From God's own ho-ly word.
'Twill be the old, old sto-ry, That I have loved so long.

REFRAIN

I love to tell the sto-ry, 'Twill be my theme in glo-ry.

I Love to Tell the Story

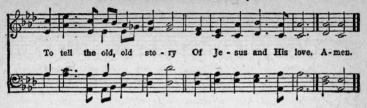

To tell the old, old sto-ry Of Je-sus and His love. A-men.

73

Fairest Lord Jesus

Crusaders' Hymn 568558

Anon. German, xvii C. Tr. Anon. 1850

In *Schlesischen Volkslieder*, 1842

1. Fair-est Lord Je-sus, Rul-er of all na-ture,
2. Fair are the mead-ows, Fair-er still the wood-lands,
3. Fair is the sun-shine, Fair-er still the moon-light,

O Thou of God and man the Son; Thee will I cher-ish,
Robed in the bloom-ing garb of spring; Je-sus is fair-er,
And all the twink-ling, star-ry host; Je-sus shines bright-er,

Thee will I hon-or, Thou, my soul's glo-ry, joy, and crown.
Je-sus is pur-er, Who makes the woe-ful heart to sing.
Je-sus shines pur-er Than all the an-gels heaven can boast. A-men.

74 More Love to Thee, O Christ

More Love to Thee 6 4 6 4 6 6 4 4

ELIZABETH P. PRENTISS, 1869

W. HOWARD DOANE, 1868

1. More love to Thee, O Christ, More love to Thee; Hear Thou the
2. Once earth-ly joy I craved, Sought peace and rest; Now Thee a-
3. Let sor-row do its work, Come grief or pain; Sweet are Thy
4. Then shall my lat-est breath Whis-per Thy praise, This be the

prayer I make On bend-ed knee; This is my ear-nest plea,
lone I seek, Give what is best; This all my prayer shall be,
mes-sen-gers, Sweet their re-frain, When they can sing with me,
part-ing cry My heart shall raise; This still its prayer shall be:

More love, O Christ, to Thee, More love to Thee, More love to Thee. A-men.

75 Fight the Good Fight

Pentecost L. M.

JOHN S. B. MONSELL, 1863

WILLIAM BOYD, 1864

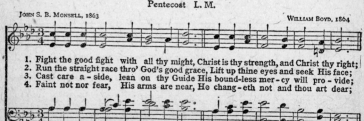

1. Fight the good fight with all thy might, Christ is thy strength, and Christ thy right;
2. Run the straight race thro' God's good grace, Lift up thine eyes and seek His face;
3. Cast care a-side, lean on thy Guide His bound-less mer-cy will pro-vide;
4. Faint not nor fear, His arms are near, He chang-eth not and thou art dear;

Fight the Good Fight

Lay hold on life, and it shall be Thy joy and crown e-ter-nal-ly.
Life with its way be-fore us lies, Christ is the path, and Christ the prize.
Trust, and thy trusting soul shall prove Christ is its life, and Christ its love.
On-ly be-lieve, and thou shalt see That Christ is all in all to thee. A-men.

76 Rock of Ages, Cleft for Me

Toplady 777777

AUGUSTUS M. TOPLADY, 1776   THOMAS HASTINGS, 1830

1. Rock of A-ges, cleft for me, Let me hide my-self in Thee;
2. Not the la-bors of my hands Can ful-fil Thy law's de-mands;
3. While I draw this fleet-ing breath, When my eye-lids close in death,

Let the wa-ter and the blood, From Thy riv-en side which flowed,
Could my zeal no res-pite know, Could my tears for-ev-er flow,
When I soar to worlds un-known, See Thee on Thy judg-ment throne,

Be of sin the dou-ble cure, Cleanse me from its guilt and power.
All for sin could not a-tone; Thou must save, and Thou a-lone.
Rock of A-ges, cleft for me, Let me hide my-self in Thee. A-men.

I Need Thee Every Hour

Need 6 4 6 4 With Refrain

ANNIE S. HAWKS, 1872   ROBERT LOWRY, 1872

1. I need Thee eve-ry hour, Most gra - cious Lord;
2. I need Thee eve-ry hour, Stay Thou near by;
3. I need Thee eve-ry hour, In joy or pain;
4. I need Thee eve-ry hour, Teach me Thy will;
5. I need Thee eve-ry hour, Most ho - ly One;

No ten - der voice like Thine Can peace af - ford.
Temp - ta - tions lose their power When Thou art nigh.
Come quick - ly and a - bide, Or life is vain.
And Thy rich prom - is - es In me ful - fil.
O make me Thine in - deed, Thou bless - ed Son.

REFRAIN

I need Thee, O I need Thee, Eve - ry hour I need Thee;

O bless me now, my Sav - iour, I come to Thee. A - men.

78 Amazing Grace

Grace C.M.

JOHN NEWTON, 1725-1807   Early American melody

1. A - maz - ing grace! how sweet the sound, That saved a wretch like me! I
2. 'Twas grace that taught my heart to fear, And grace my fears re-lieved; How
3. Thro' man - y dan-gers, toils and snares, I have al - read - y come; 'Tis
4. When we've been there ten thou-sand years Bright shin-ing as the sun, We've

once was lost, but now am found, Was blind, but now I see.
pre - cious did that grace ap - pear The hour I first be-lieved!!
grace hath bro't me safe thus far, And grace will lead me home.
no less days to sing God's praise Than when we first be - gun. A - men.

79 I Can Hear My Savior Calling

Where He Leads Me 8889

E. W. BLANDLY   J. S. NORRIS

1. I can hear my Sav - ior call-ing, I can hear my Sav - ior call-ing,
2. I'll go with Him thro' the gar-den, I'll go with Him thro' the gar-den,
3. I'll go with Him thro' the judgment, I'll go with Him thro' the judgment,
4. He will give me grace and glo - ry, He will give me grace and glo - ry,

REF. Where He leads me I will fol-low, Where He leads me I will fol-low,

I can hear my Sav - ior call-ing, "Take thy cross and fol-low, fol - low Me."
I'll go with Him thro' the gar-den, I'll go with Him, with Him all the way.
I'll go with Him thro' the judgment, I'll go with Him, with Him all the way.
He will give me grace and glo - ry, And go with me, with me all the way.

Where He leads me I will fol-low, I'll go with Him, with Him all the way. A-men.

80 There's a Dear and Precious Book

My Mother's Bible 7 7 11 D With Refrain

M. B. Williams
DUET

Charlie D. Tillman, 1893

1. There's a dear and precious book, Tho' it's worn and fad-ed now, Which re-
2. There she read of Je-sus' love, As he blest the chil-dren dear, How he
3. Well, those days are past and gone, But their mem-'ry lin-gers still, And the

calls the hap-py days of long a-go; When I stood at mother's knee,
suffered, bled and died up-on the tree; Of his heav-y load and care,
dear old Book each day has been my guide; And I seek to do his will,

With her hand up-on my brow, And I heard her voice in gentle tones and low.
Then she dried my flowing tear, With her kisses as she said it was for me.
As my moth-er taught me then, And ev-er in my heart his words abide.

REFRAIN

Bless-ed book, precious book, On thy dear old tear-stain'd
Bless-ed book, precious book,

leaves I love to look; Thou art sweet-er day by day, As I
love to look;

Copyright, 1921, Renewal, by Charlie D. Tillman. Used by permission.

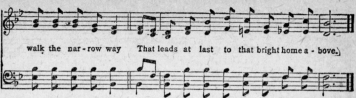

There's a Dear and Precious Book

walk the nar-row way   That leads at last   to that bright home a - bove.

81   I Hear Thy Welcome Voice

Welcome Voice   S. M. With Refrain

Lewis Hartsough   Lewis Hartsough

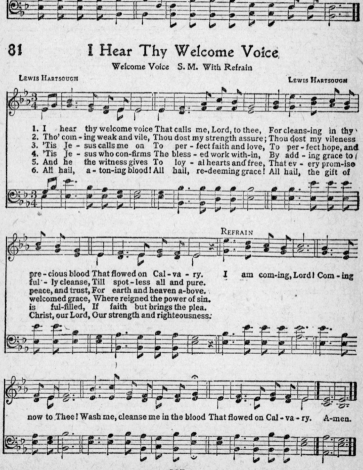

1. I   hear   thy welcome voice That calls me, Lord, to thee,   For cleans-ing in thy
2. Tho' com - ing weak and vile, Thou dost my strength assure; Thou dost my vileness
3. 'Tis Je - sus calls me on   To   per - fect faith and love,   To per - fect hope, and
4. 'Tis Je - sus who con-firms The bless - ed work with-in,   By add - ing grace to
5. And he   the witness gives To   loy - al hearts and free, That ev - ery prom-ise
6. All hail,   a - ton-ing blood! All   hail, re-deeming grace! All hail, the gift of

Refrain

pre - cious blood That flowed on Cal - va - ry.   I   am com-ing, Lord! Com-ing
ful - ly cleanse, Till spot - less all and pure.
peace, and trust, For   earth and heaven a-bove.
welcomed grace, Where reigned the power of sin.
is   ful-filled, If   faith but brings the plea.
Christ, our Lord, Our strength and righteousness.

now to Thee! Wash me, cleanse me in the blood That flowed on Cal - va - ry.   A-men.

82 Yield Not to Temptation

Palmer 10 10 10 10 With Refrain

HORATIO R. PALMER, 1868

HORATIO R. PALMER, 1868

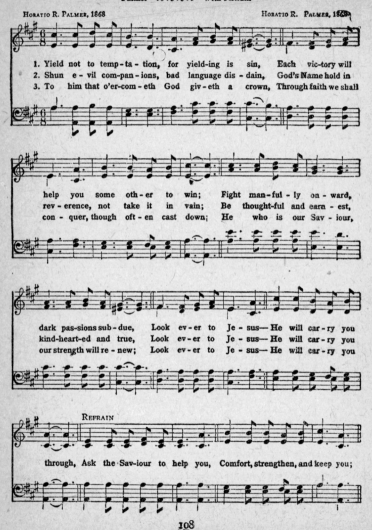

1. Yield not to temp-ta-tion, for yield-ing is sin, Each vic-tory will
2. Shun e-vil com-pan-ions, bad language dis-dain, God's Name hold in
3. To him that o'er-com-eth God giv-eth a crown, Through faith we shall

help you some oth-er to win; Fight man-ful-ly on-ward,
rev-erence, not take it in vain; Be thought-ful and earn-est,
con-quer, though oft-en cast down; He who is our Sav-iour,

dark pas-sions sub-due, Look ev-er to Je-sus— He will car-ry you
kind-heart-ed and true, Look ev-er to Je-sus— He will car-ry you
our strength will re-new; Look ev-er to Je-sus— He will car-ry you

REFRAIN

through, Ask the Sav-iour to help you, Comfort, strengthen, and keep you;

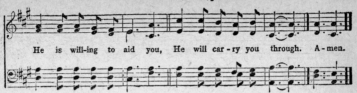

Yield Not to Temptation

He is will-ing to aid you, He will car-ry you through. A-men.

---

83   Come, Thou Fount of Every Blessing

Nettleton 87878787

ROBERT ROBINSON, 1758

JOHN WYETH, 1812

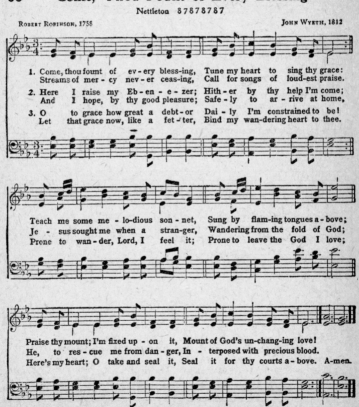

1. Come, thou fount of ev - ery bless-ing,   Tune my heart to sing thy grace:
   Streams of mer - cy nev - er ceas-ing,   Call for songs of loud-est praise.

2. Here I raise my Eb - en - e - zer;   Hith - er by thy help I'm come;
   And I hope, by thy good pleasure;   Safe - ly to ar - rive at home,

3. O to grace how great a debt - or   Dai - ly I'm constrained to be!
   Let that grace now, like a fet - ter,   Bind my wan-dering heart to thee.

Teach me some me - lo-dious son - net,   Sung by flam-ing tongues a - bove;
Je - sus sought me when a stran-ger,   Wandering from the fold of God;
Prone to wan - der, Lord, I feel it;   Prone to leave the God I love;

Praise thy mount; I'm fixed up - on it,   Mount of God's un-chang-ing love!
He, to res - cue me from dan - ger, In - terposed with precious blood.
Here's my heart; O take and seal it,   Seal it for thy courts a - bove. A-men.

In the Hour of Trial

Penitence 6 5 6 5 D

J. Montgomery, 1834
Alt. Frances A. Hutton and Godfrey Thring

Spencer Lane, 1879

1. In the hour of tri - al, Je - sus plead for me,
2. With for - bid - den pleas - ures Would this vain world charm,
3. Should Thy mer - cy send me Sor - row, toil, and woe,
4. When my last hour com - eth, Fraught with strife and pain,

Lest by base de - ni - al I de - part from Thee;
Or its sor - did treas - ures Spread to work me harm;
Or should pain at - tend me On my path be - low;
When my dust re - turn - eth To the dust a - gain;

When Thou see'st me wav - er, With a look re - call,
Bring to my re - mem - brance Sad Geth - sem - a - ne,
Grant that I may nev - er Fail Thy hand to see;
On Thy truth re - ly - ing, Through that mor - tal strife,

Nor, for fear or fa - vor, Suf - fer me to fall.
Or, in dark - er sem - blance, Cross-crowned Cal - va - ry.
Grant that I may ev - er Cast my care on Thee.
Je - sus, take me, dy - ing, To e - ter - nal life. A - men.

Stand up, Stand up for Jesus

Webb 7 6 7 6 D

GEORGE DUFFIELD, 1858

GEORGE J. WEBB, 1837

1. Stand up, stand up for Je - sus, Ye sol - diers of the cross,
2. Stand up, stand up for Je - sus, The trum - pet call o - bey,
3. Stand up, stand up for Je - sus, Stand in His strength a - lone;
4. Stand up, stand up for Je - sus, The strife will not be long;

Lift high His roy - al ban - ner, It must not suf - fer loss;
Forth to the might - y con - flict In this His glo - rious day;
The arm of flesh will fail you, Ye dare not trust your own;
This day the noise of bat - tle, The next the vic - tor's song;

From vic - tory un - to vic - tory His ar - my He shall lead,
Ye that are men now serve Him A - gainst un - num - bered foes;
Put on the gos - pel ar - mor, Each piece put on with prayer;
To him that o - ver - com - eth A crown of life shall be,

Till eve - ry foe is van-quished, And Christ is Lord in - deed.
Let cour - age rise with dan - ger, And strength to strength op - pose.
Where du - ty calls, or dan - ger, Be nev - er want - ing there.
He with the King of Glo - ry Shall reign e - ter - nal - ly. A-men.

Onward, Christian Soldiers

St. Gertrude 6 5 6 5 D With Refrain

S. BARING-GOULD, 1865

ARTHUR SULLIVAN, 1871

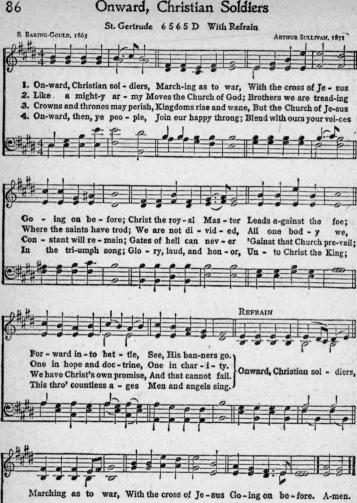

1. On-ward, Christian sol - diers, March-ing as to war, With the cross of Je - sus
2. Like a might-y ar - my Moves the Church of God; Brothers we are tread-ing
3. Crowns and thrones may perish, Kingdoms rise and wane, But the Church of Je-sus
4. On-ward, then, ye peo - ple, Join our happy throng; Blend with ours your voi-ces

Go - ing on be - fore; Christ the roy - al Mas - ter Leads a-gainst the foe;
Where the saints have trod; We are not di - vid - ed, All one bod - y we,
Con - stant will re - main; Gates of hell can nev - er 'Gainst that Church pre-vail;
In the tri-umph song; Glo - ry, laud, and hon - or, Un - to Christ the King;

REFRAIN

For - ward in-to bat - tle, See, His ban-ners go.
One in hope and doc - trine, One in char - i - ty.   Onward, Christian sol - diers,
We have Christ's own promise, And that cannot fail.
This thro' countless a - ges Men and angels sing.

Marching as to war, With the cross of Je - sus Go-ing on be - fore. A-men.

Work, for the Night is Coming

Work Song 7675 D

Anna L. Coghill, c. 1854

Lowell Mason, 1864

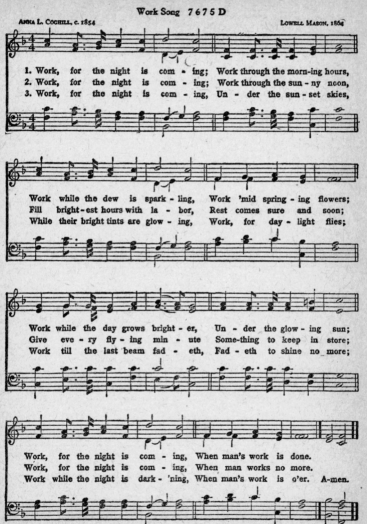

1. Work, for the night is com - ing; Work through the morn-ing hours,
2. Work, for the night is com - ing; Work through the sun - ny noon,
3. Work, for the night is com - ing, Un - der the sun - set skies,

Work while the dew is spark - ling, Work 'mid spring - ing flowers;
Fill bright - est hours with la - bor, Rest comes sure and soon;
While their bright tints are glow - ing, Work, for day - light flies;

Work while the day grows bright - er, Un - der the glow - ing sun;
Give eve - ry fly - ing min - ute Some-thing to keep in store;
Work till the last beam fad - eth, Fad - eth to shine no more;

Work, for the night is com - ing, When man's work is done.
Work, for the night is com - ing, When man works no more.
Work while the night is dark - 'ning, When man's work is o'er. A-men.

Lead on, O King Eternal

Lancashire 7676 D

Ernest W. Shurtleff, 1888

Henry Smart, 1835

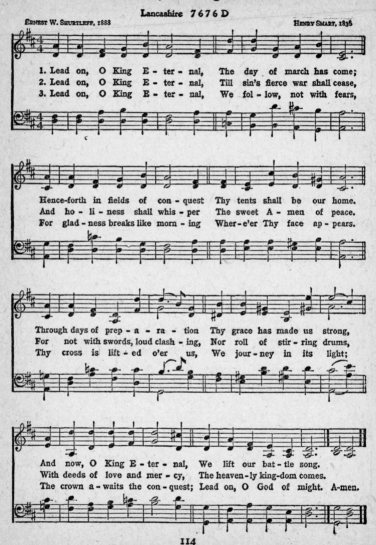

1. Lead on, O King E-ter-nal, The day of march has come;
Hence-forth in fields of con-quest Thy tents shall be our home.
Through days of prep-a-ra-tion Thy grace has made us strong,
And now, O King E-ter-nal, We lift our bat-tle song.

2. Lead on, O King E-ter-nal, Till sin's fierce war shall cease,
And ho-li-ness shall whis-per The sweet A-men of peace.
For not with swords, loud clash-ing, Nor roll of stir-ring drums,
With deeds of love and mer-cy, The heaven-ly king-dom comes.

3. Lead on, O King E-ter-nal, We fol-low, not with fears,
For glad-ness breaks like morn-ing Wher-e'er Thy face ap-pears.
Thy cross is lift-ed o'er us, We jour-ney in its light;
The crown a-waits the con-quest; Lead on, O God of might. A-men.

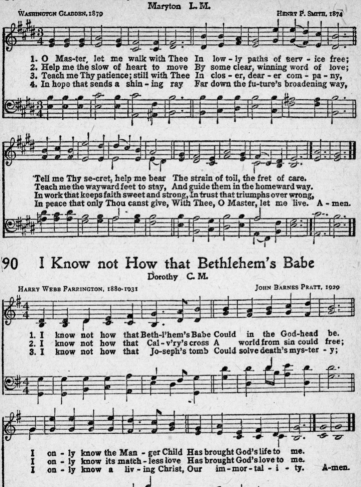

Harvard Prize-Hymn, Copyright, 1924, Harry Webb Farrington.
Tune copyright. 1939, by A. S. Barnes and Company, Inc.

91.
Praise Him! Praise Him
Irregular

FANNY J. CROSBY, 1820-1915

CHESTER G. ALLEN

1. Praise him! praise him! Je-sus, our bless-ed Re-deem-er!
2. Praise him! praise him! Je-sus, our bless-ed Re-deem-er!
3. Praise him! praise him! Je-sus, our bless-ed Re-deem-er!

Sing, O earth—his won-der-ful love pro-claim! Hail him! hail him!
For our sins he suffered, and bled, and died; He our Rock, our
Heavenly por-tals loud with ho-san-nas ring! Je-sus, Sav-iour,

Praise him! praise him!

high-est arch-an-gels in glo-ry; Strength and hon-or
hope of e-ter-nal sal-va-tion, Hail him! hail him!
reign-eth for-ev-er and ev-er; Crown him! crown him!

tell of his ex-cel-lent great-ness, Praise him! praise him!

Fine

give to his ho-ly name! Like a shepherd Je-sus will guard his
Je-sus, the Cru-ci-fied, Sound his prais-es! Je-sus who bore our
Prophet, and Priest, and King! Christ is com-ing! o-ver the world vic-

ev-er in joy-ful song!

D. S.

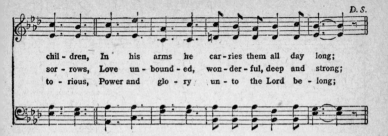

chil - dren, In his arms he car - ries them all day long;
sor - rows, Love un - bound - ed, won - der - ful, deep and strong;
to - rious, Power and glo - ry un - to the Lord be - long;

92   Am I a Soldier of the Cross

Arlington   C. M.

Isaac Watts, 1674-1748   Thomas A. Arne, 1710-1778

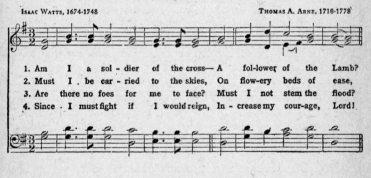

1. Am I a sol - dier of the cross— A fol-lower of the Lamb?
2. Must I be car - ried to the skies, On flow-ery beds of ease,
3. Are there no foes for me to face? Must I not stem the flood?
4. Since I must fight if I would reign, In - crease my cour-age, Lord!

And shall I fear to own his cause, Or blush to speak his name?
While oth - ers fought to win the prize, And sailed thro' bloody seas?
Is this vile world a friend to grace, To help me on to God?
I'll bear the toil, en - dure the pain, Sup - port - ed by thy word. A - men.

93 Jesus, I my Cross Have Taken

Ellesdie 8 7 8 7 D

Henry F. Lyte, 1824

Arr. fr. W. A. Mozart, by Hubert P. Main, 1873

1. Je - sus, I my cross have tak - en, All to leave, and fol - low Thee;
2. Take, my soul, thy full sal - va - tion, Rise o'er sin, and fear, and care;
3. Haste, then, on from grace to glo - ry, Armed by faith and winged by prayer;

Des - ti - tute, de - spised, for-sak - en, Thou, from hence, my all shalt be.
Joy to find in eve - ry sta - tion Some-thing still to do or bear.
Heaven's e-ter - nal day's be - fore Thee, God's own hand shall guide thee there.

Per - ish eve - ry fond am - bi - tion, All I've sought, and hoped, or known;
Think what Spir - it dwells with - in thee, What a Fa - ther's smile is thine,
Soon shall close thy earth - ly mis - sion; Swift shall pass thy pil - grim's days;

Yet how rich is my con - di - tion, God and heaven are still my own.
What a Sav - iour died to win thee,—Child of heaven, shouldst thou re-pine?
Hope should change to glad fru-i-tion, Faith to sight, and prayer to praise. A-men.

94 Sweet Hour of Prayer

Sweet Hour L. M. D.

W. W. WALFORD

W. B. BRADBURY, 1816-1868

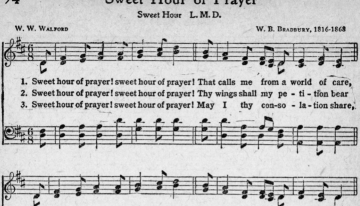

1. Sweet hour of prayer! sweet hour of prayer! That calls me from a world of care,
2. Sweet hour of prayer! sweet hour of prayer! Thy wings shall my pe - ti - tion bear
3. Sweet hour of prayer! sweet hour of prayer! May I thy con - so - la - tion share,

And bid me at my Fa-ther's throne Make all my wants and wish-es known;
To him whose truth and faith - ful-ness En - gage the wait-ing soul to bless.
Till, from Mount Pisgah's loft - y height, I view my home and take my flight;

In sea - sons of dis - tress and grief, My soul has oft - en found re - lief;
And since he bids me seek his face, Be - lieve his word and trust his grace,
This robe of flesh I'll drop, and rise To seize the ev - er - last - ing prize;

And oft escaped the tempter's snare, By thy re-turn, sweet hour of prayer!
I'll cast on him my ev - ery care And wait for thee, sweet hour of prayer!
And shout, while passing thro' the air, Farewell, farewell, sweet hour of prayer! A-men.

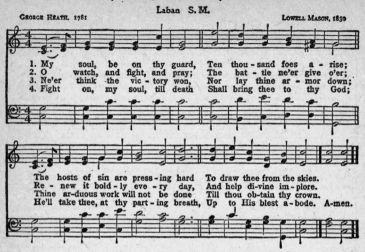

95

My Soul, be on thy Guard

Laban S.M.

GEORGE HEATH. 1781

LOWELL MASON. 1830

1. My soul, be on thy guard, Ten thou-sand foes a - rise;
2. O watch, and fight, and pray; The bat - tle ne'er give o'er;
3. Ne'er think the vic-to-ry won, Nor lay thine ar - mor down;
4. Fight on, my soul, till death Shall bring thee to thy God;

The hosts of sin are press-ing hard To draw thee from the skies.
Re - new it bold-ly ev-e-ry day, And help di-vine im-plore.
Thine ar-duous work will not be done Till thou ob-tain thy crown.
He'll take thee, at thy part-ing breath, Up to His blest a-bode. A-men.

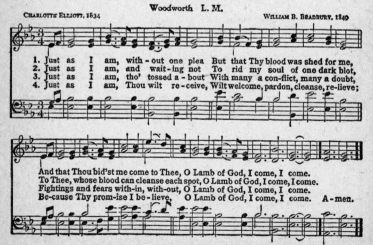

96

Just as I am, Without One Plea

Woodworth L.M.

CHARLOTTE ELLIOTT. 1834

WILLIAM B. BRADBURY. 1849

1. Just as I am, with-out one plea But that Thy blood was shed for me,
2. Just as I am, and wait-ing not To rid my soul of one dark blot,
3. Just as I am, tho' tossed a-bout With many a con-flict, many a doubt,
4. Just as I am, Thou wilt re-ceive, Wilt welcome, pardon, cleanse, re-lieve;

And that Thou bid'st me come to Thee, O Lamb of God, I come, I come.
To Thee, whose blood can cleanse each spot, O Lamb of God, I come, I come.
Fightings and fears with-in, with-out, O Lamb of God, I come, I come.
Be-cause Thy prom-ise I be-lieve, O Lamb of God, I come, I come. A-men.

What a Friend we Have in Jesus

Erie 8 7 8 7 D

JOSEPH SCRIVEN, 1855

CHARLES C. CONVERSE, 1868

1. What a friend we have in Je - sus,   All   our sins and griefs to bear;
2. Have we tri - als and temp-ta - tions?   Is   there trou-ble an - y - where?
3. Are   we weak and heav-y - la - den,   Cum-bered with a load of care?

What a priv - i - lege to car - ry   Eve - ry-thing to God in prayer!
We should nev-er be dis - cour - aged;   Take it to the Lord in prayer.
Pre - cious Sav-iour, still our ref - uge;   Take it to the Lord in prayer.

O   what peace we oft - en   for - feit,   O   what need-less pain we bear,
Can   we find a friend so faith - ful,   Who will all our sor - rows share?
Do   thy friends despise, for - sake thee?   Take it to the Lord in prayer;

All   be-cause we do not car - ry   Eve - ry-thing to God in prayer.
Je - sus knows our eve-ry weak-ness;   Take it to the Lord in prayer.
In   His arms He'll take and shield thee, Thou wilt find a sol - ace there.   A - men.

Jesus Calls us, O'er the Tumult

Galilee 8787

CECIL F. ALEXANDER, 1852

WILLIAM H. JUDE, 1874

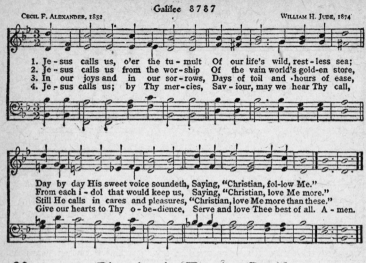

1. Je-sus calls us, o'er the tu-mult Of our life's wild, rest-less sea;
2. Je-sus calls us from the wor-ship Of the vain world's gold-en store,
3. In our joys and in our sor-rows, Days of toil and hours of ease,
4. Je-sus calls us; by Thy mer-cies, Sav-iour, may we hear Thy call,

Day by day His sweet voice soundeth, Saying, "Christian, fol-low Me."
From each i-dol that would keep us, Saying, "Christian, love Me more."
Still He calls in cares and pleasures, "Christian, love Me more than these."
Give our hearts to Thy o-be-dience, Serve and love Thee best of all. A-men.

Blest be the Tie that Binds

Dennis S. M.

JOHN FAWCETT, 1740-1817

From HANS G. NÄGELI, 1768-1836
Arr. by LOWELL MASON, 1792-1872

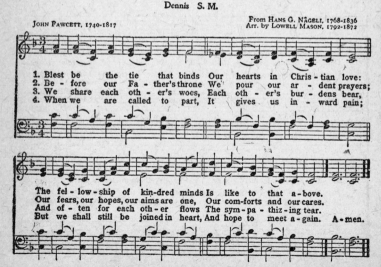

1. Blest be the tie that binds Our hearts in Chris-tian love:
2. Be-fore our Fa-ther's throne We pour our ar-dent prayers;
3. We share each oth-er's woes, Each oth-er's bur-dens bear,
4. When we are called to part, It gives us in-ward pain;

The fel-low-ship of kin-dred minds Is like to that a-bove.
Our fears, our hopes, our aims are one, Our com-forts and our cares.
And of-ten for each oth-er flows The sym-pa-thiz-ing tear.
But we shall still be joined in heart, And hope to meet a-gain. A-men.

100 Jesus Is Tenderly Calling

Calling Today   10 8 10 7   With Refrain

FANNY J. CROSBY, 1820-1915

GEO. C. STEBBINS, 1846-

1. Je-sus is ten-der-ly call-ing thee home—Call-ing to-day, call-ing to-day;
2. Je-sus is call-ing the wea-ry to rest—Call-ing to-day, call-ing to-day;
3. Je-sus is wait-ing, oh, come to him now—Waiting to-day, wait-ing to-day;
4. Je-sus is pleading, oh, list to his voice—Hear him to-day, hear him to-day;

Why from the sun-shine of love wilt thou roam Far-ther and far-ther a-way?
Bring him thy bur-den, and thou shalt be blest; He will not turn thee a-way.
Come with thy sins, at his feet low-ly bow; Come, and no lon-ger de-lay.
They who be-lieve on his name shall re-joice; Quickly a-rise and a-way.

REFRAIN

Call - - ing to-day!   Call - - ing to-day!
Call-ing, call-ing to-day, to-day;   Call-ing, call-ing to-day, to-day;

Je - - sus is call - - ing, Is ten-der-ly call-ing to-day.   A-men.
Je-sus is ten-der-ly call-ing to-day.

101 Break Thou the Bread of Life

Bread of Life 6 4 6 4 D

MARY A. LATHBURY, 1877
WILLIAM F SHERWIN, 1877

1. Break Thou the bread of life, Dear Lord, to me, As Thou didst
break the loaves Be - side the sea; Be - yond the sa - cred page
I seek Thee, Lord, My spir - it pants for Thee, O liv - ing Word.

2. Bless Thou the truth, dear Lord, To me, to me, As Thou didst
bless the bread By Gal - i - lee; Then shall all bond - age cease,
All fet - ters fall, And I shall find my peace, My All in all. A-men.

102 O For a Faith

Evan C. M.

WILLIAM H. BATHURST, 1831
REV. W. H. HAVERGAL, 1793-1870

1. O for a faith that will not shrink, Though pressed by ev - ery foe,
2. That will not mur - mur nor com-plain Be - neath the chast-ening rod,
3. A faith that shines more bright and clear When tem-pests rage with - out;
4. Lord, give us such a faith as this, And then, what-e'er may come,

O for a Faith

That will not trem-ble   on the brink   Of an-y earth-ly woe;
But, in the hour of   grief and pain,   Will lean up-on   its God;
That, when in dan-ger, knows no fear,   In dark-ness feels   no doubt.
We'll taste, e'en here, the   hal-lowed bliss   Of an e-ter-nal home.

103

Jesus, Saviour Pilot Me

Pilot 7 7 7 7 7 7

EDWARD HOPPER, 1871   JOHN E. GOULD. 1871

1. Je - sus, Sav - iour, pi - lot me   O - ver life's tem-pest-uous sea;
2. As a moth - er stills her child,   Thou canst hush the o - cean wild;
3. When at last   I near the shore,   And the fear - ful break-ers roar

Un-known waves be-fore me roll,   Hid - ing rock and treach-'rous shoals;
Bois-terous waves o - bey Thy will   When Thou sayest to them, "Be still."
'Twixt me and the peace-ful rest,   Then, while lean-ing on Thy breast,

Chart and com-pass came from Thee: Je - sus, Sav - iour, pi - lot me.
Won - drous Sov-ereign of the sea, Je - sus, Sav - iour, pi - lot me.
May   I hear Thee say to me, "Fear not, I will pi - lot thee." A-men.

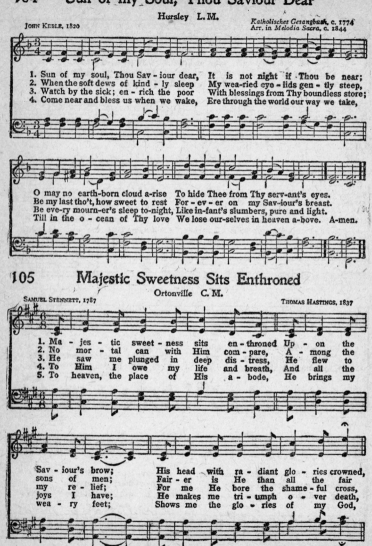

104 — Sun of my Soul, Thou Saviour Dear

Hursley L. M.

JOHN KEBLE, 1820

Katholisches Gesangbuch, c. 1774
Arr. in Melodia Sacra, c. 1844

1. Sun of my soul, Thou Sav - iour dear, It is not night if Thou be near;
2. When the soft dews of kind - ly sleep My wea-ried eye - lids gen - tly steep,
3. Watch by the sick; en - rich the poor With blessings from Thy boundless store;
4. Come near and bless us when we wake, Ere through the world our way we take,

O may no earth-born cloud a-rise To hide Thee from Thy serv-ant's eyes.
Be my last tho't, how sweet to rest For - ev - er on my Sav-iour's breast.
Be eve-ry mourn-er's sleep to-night, Like in-fant's slumbers, pure and light.
Till in the o - cean of Thy love We lose our-selves in heaven a-bove. A-men.

105 — Majestic Sweetness Sits Enthroned

Ortonville C. M.

SAMUEL STENNETT, 1787

THOMAS HASTINGS, 1837

1. Ma - jes - tic sweet - ness sits en - throned Up - on the
2. No mor - tal can with Him com - pare, A - mong the
3. He saw me plunged in deep dis - tress, He flew to
4. To Him I owe my life and breath, And all the
5. To heaven, the place of His a - bode, He brings my

Sav - iour's brow; His head with ra - diant glo - ries crowned,
sons of men; Fair - er is He than all the fair
my re - lief; For me He bore the shame - ful cross,
joys I have; He makes me tri - umph o - ver death,
wea - ry feet; Shows me the glo - ries of my God,

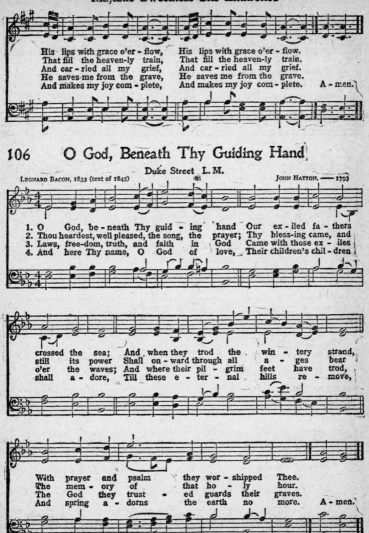

Majestic Sweetness Sits Enthroned

His lips with grace o'er - flow,   His lips with grace o'er - flow.
That fill the heaven-ly train,   That fill the heaven-ly train.
And car - ried all my grief,   And car - ried all my grief.
He saves me from the grave,   He saves me from the grave.
And makes my joy com - plete,   And makes my joy com - plete.   A - men.

106   O God, Beneath Thy Guiding Hand

Duke Street. L. M.

LEONARD BACON, 1833 (text of 1845)   JOHN HATTON. —— 1793

1. O   God, be - neath Thy guid - ing hand   Our ex - iled fa - thers
2. Thou heardest, well pleased, the song, the   prayer; Thy bless-ing came, and
3. Laws, free-dom, truth, and faith in   God   Came with those ex - iles
4. And   here Thy name, O   God   of   love,   Their children's chil - dren

crossed the sea;   And when they trod   the   win - tery   strand,
still   its power Shall on - ward through all   a - ges   bear
o'er   the   waves; And where their pil - grim   feet   have   trod,
shall   a - dore,   Till these e - ter - nal   hills   re - move,

With   prayer   and   psalm   they wor - shipped   Thee.
The   mem - ory   of   that ho - ly   hour.
The   God   they   trust - ed   guards   their   graves.
And   spring   a - dorns   the   earth   no   more.   A - men.

127

107 I've Found a Friend

Constance 8 7 8 7 D

James G. Small, 1863

Arthur Sullivan, 1873

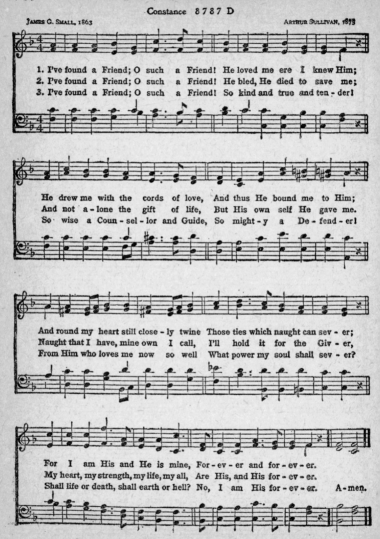

1. I've found a Friend; O such a Friend! He loved me ere I knew Him;
2. I've found a Friend; O such a Friend! He bled, He died to save me;
3. I've found a Friend; O such a Friend! So kind and true and ten - der!

He drew me with the cords of love, And thus He bound me to Him;
And not a - lone the gift of life, But His own self He gave me.
So wise a Coun - sel - lor and Guide, So might - y a De - fend - er!

And round my heart still close - ly twine Those ties which naught can sev - er;
Naught that I have, mine own I call, I'll hold it for the Giv - er,
From Him who loves me now so well What power my soul shall sev - er?

For I am His and He is mine, For - ev - er and for - ev - er.
My heart, my strength, my life, my all, Are His, and His for - ev - er.
Shall life or death, shall earth or hell? No, I am His for - ev - er. A - men.

I Would be True

Peek 11 10 11 10

Howard A. Walter, 1883-1918

J. Yates Peek

1. I would be true, for there are those who trust me;
2. I would be friend of all, the foe, the friend-less;

I would be pure, for there are those who care; I would be
I would be giv-ing, and for-get the gift; I would be

strong, for there is much to suf-fer; I would be brave, for
hum-ble, for I know my weak-ness; I would look up, and

there is much to dare, I would be brave, for there is much to dare.
laugh, and love and lift, I would look up, and laugh, and love, and lift. A-men.

Jesus Keep Me Near the Cross

Near the Cross 7676 With Refrain

FANNY J. CROSBY, 1820-1915

W. HOWARD DOANE, 1868

1. Je - sus, keep me near the cross,   There a pre - cious foun - tain
2. Near the cross, a tremb - ling soul   Love and mer - cy found me;
3. Near the cross, O Lamb of God!   Bring its scenes be - fore me;
4. Near the cross I'll watch and wait;   Hop - ing, trust - ing ev - er,

Free to all, a heal - ing stream,   Flows from Cal - vary's moun - tain.
There the Bright and Morn - ing Star   Sheds its beams a - round me.
Help me walk from day to day,   With its shad - ows o'er me.
Till I reach the gold - en strand,   Just be - yond the riv - er.

REFRAIN

In the cross, in the cross   Be my glo - ry ev - er;

Till my rap - tured soul shall find   Rest be - yond the riv - er.   A - men.

110 Be Still, My Soul

Findlandia 10 10 10 10 10 10

Katharina von Schlegel, born 1697
Trans. by Jane Laurie Borthwick, 1813-1897

Arr. from Jean Sibelius, 1865.

In moderate time. May be sung in unison.

1. Be still, my soul: the Lord is on thy side;
   Bear patiently the cross of grief or pain; Leave to thy God to order and provide;
   In every change He faithful will remain.
   Be still, my soul: thy best, thy heavenly Friend Through thorny ways leads to a joyful end.

2. Be still, my soul: thy God doth undertake
   To guide the future as He has the past. Thy hope, thy confidence let nothing shake;
   All now mysterious shall be bright at last.
   Be still, my soul: the waves and winds still know His voice who ruled them while He dwelt below.

3. Be still, my soul: the hour is hastening on
   When we shall be forever with the Lord, When disappointment, grief, and fear are gone,
   Sorrow forgot, love's purest joys restored.
   Be still, my soul: when change and tears are past, All safe and blessed we shall meet at last. A-men.

Music used by permission of The Presbyterian Board of Christian Education, owner of the special arrangement made in 1932.

111 Safely Through Another Week

Sabbath 777777

JOHN NEWTON, 1774

LOWELL MASON, 1824

1. Safe-ly through an-oth-er week, God has brought us on our way;
2. While we pray for pardon-ing grace, Thro' the dear Re-deem-er's name,
3. Here we come Thy name to praise, May we feel Thy pres-ence near;
4. May Thy gos-pel's joy-ful sound Con-quer sin-ners, com-fort saints;

Let us now a bless-ing seek, Wait-ing in His courts to-day:
Show Thy rec-on-cil-ed face; Take a-way our sin and shame:
May Thy glo-ry meet our eyes, While we in Thy house ap-pear:
May the fruits of grace a-bound, Bring re-lief for all com-plaints:

Day of all the week the best, Em-blem of e-ter-nal rest;
From our world-ly cares set free, May we rest this day in Thee;
Here af-ford us, Lord, a taste Of our ev-er-last-ing feast;
Thus may all our Sab-baths prove Till we join the Church a-bove;

Day of all the week the best, Em-blem of e-ter-nal rest.
From our world-ly cares set free, May we rest this day in Thee.
Here af-ford us, Lord, a taste Of our ev-er-last-ing feast.
Thus may all our Sab-baths prove Till we join the Church a-bove. A-men.

112 Come, Thou Almighty King

Italian Hymn 6 6 4 6 6 6 4

Anonymous, c. 1757

With reverence. Unhurried.

Felice de Giardini, 1769

1. Come, Thou al-might-y King, Help us Thy name to sing, Help us to praise; Fa-ther, all glo-ri-ous, O'er all vic-to-ri-ous, Come and reign o-ver us, An-cient of Days.

2. Come, Thou in-car-nate Word, Gird on Thy sword, Our prayer at-tend; Come, and Thy peo-ple bless, And give Thy word suc-cess; Spir-it of ho-li-ness, On us de-scend.

3. Come, ho-ly Com-fort-er, Thy sa-cred wit-ness bear, In this glad hour; Thou, who al-might-y art, Now rule in eve-ry heart, And ne'er from us de-part, Spir-it of power.

4. To the great One in Three E-ter-nal prais-es be, Hence ev-er-more; His sov-ereign maj-es-ty May we in glo-ry see, And to e-ter-ni-ty Love and a-dore. A-men.

133

I am Thine, O Lord

Crosby 10 7 10 7 With Refrain

Fanny J. Crosby, 1875

W. Howard Doane, 1875

1. I am Thine, O Lord, I have heard Thy voice, And it told Thy love to me; But I long to rise in the arms of faith, And be clos-er drawn to Thee.
2. Con - se - crate me now to Thy serv - ice, Lord, By the power of grace di - vine; Let my soul look up with a stead-fast hope, And my will be lost in Thine.
3. O the pure de - light of a sin - gle hour That be - fore Thy throne I spend, When I kneel in prayer, and with Thee, my God, I com-mune as friend with friend.
4. There are depths of love that I can - not know Till I cross the nar - row sea; There are heights of joy that I may not reach Till I rest in peace with Thee.

REFRAIN

Draw me near - er, nearer, blessed Lord,

Near - er, near - er,

To the cross where Thou hast died; Draw me near - er, near - er

near - er, bless-ed Lord, To Thy pre - cious bleed - ing side. A-men.

Softly and Tenderly Jesus is Calling

Thompson 11 7 11 7 With Refrain

WILL L. THOMPSON   WILL L. THOMPSON

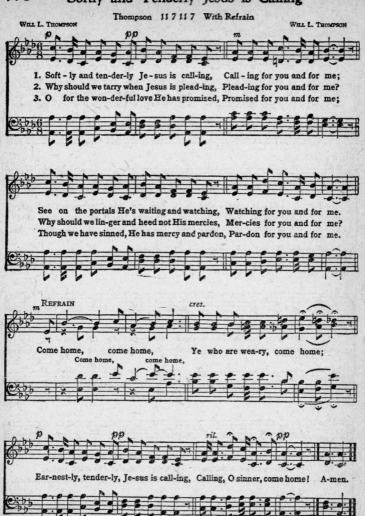

1. Soft - ly and ten-der-ly Je - sus is call-ing, Call - ing for you and for me;
2. Why should we tarry when Jesus is plead-ing, Plead-ing for you and for me?
3. O for the won-der-ful love He has promised, Promised for you and for me;

See on the portals He's waiting and watching, Watching for you and for me.
Why should we lin-ger and heed not His mercies, Mer-cies for you and for me?
Though we have sinned, He has mercy and pardon, Par-don for you and for me.

REFRAIN   cres.

Come home,   come home,   Ye who are wea-ry, come home;
    Come home,   come home,

Ear-nest-ly, tender-ly, Je-sus is call-ing, Calling, O sinner, come home! A-men.

Come, Ye Thankful People, Come

St. George's, Windsor 7 7 7 7 D

HENRY ALFORD, 1844.
Altered by HUGH HARTSHORNE, 1915

GEORGE J. ELVEY, 1859

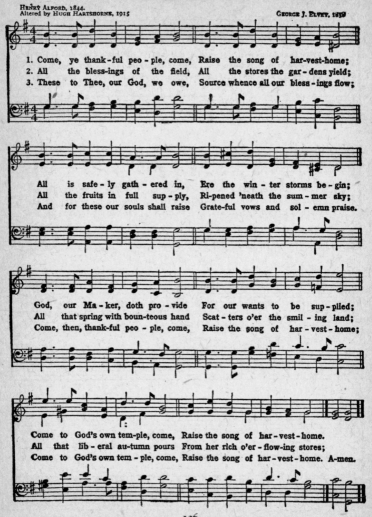

1. Come, ye thank-ful peo - ple, come, Raise the song of har-vest-home;
2. All the bless-ings of the field, All the stores the gar-dens yield;
3. These to Thee, our God, we owe, Source whence all our bless-ings flow;

All is safe - ly gath - ered in, Ere the win - ter storms be - gin;
All the fruits in full sup - ply, Ri-pened 'neath the sum - mer sky;
And for these our souls shall raise Grate-ful vows and sol - emn praise.

God, our Ma - ker, doth pro - vide For our wants to be sup - plied;
All that spring with boun-teous hand Scat-ters o'er the smil - ing land;
Come, then, thank-ful peo - ple, come, Raise the song of har - vest - home;

Come to God's own tem-ple, come, Raise the song of har-vest-home.
All that lib - er-al au-tumn pours From her rich o'er - flow-ing stores;
Come to God's own tem - ple, come, Raise the song of har - vest-home. A-men.

Jesus, Lover of my Soul

Martyn 7777 D

CHARLES WESLEY, 1740   SIMEON B. MARSH, 1834

1. Je - sus, Lov - er of my soul,   Let me to Thy bo - som fly,
2. Oth - er ref - uge have I none,   Hangs my help - less soul on Thee;
3. Thou, O Christ, art all I want,   More than all in Thee I find;
4. Plenteous grace with Thee is found,   Grace to cov - er all my sin;

While the near - er wa - ters roll, While the tem - pest still is high;
Leave, ah, leave me not a - lone, Still sup - port and com - fort me.
Raise the fall - en, cheer the faint, Heal the sick, and lead the blind.
Let the heal - ing streams a - bound, Make and keep me pure with - in.

Hide me, O my Sav - iour, hide, Till the storm of life be past;
All my trust on Thee is stayed, All my help from Thee I bring;
Just and ho - ly is Thy name, I am all un - right - eous - ness;
Thou of life the foun - tain art, Free - ly let me take of Thee;

Safe in - to the ha - ven guide, O re - ceive my soul at last.
Cov - er my de - fence-less head With the shad - ow of Thy wing.
False and full of sin I am, Thou art full of truth and grace.
Spring Thou up with - in my heart, Rise to all e - ter - ni - ty. A - men.

117 How Firm a Foundation, ye Saints

Portugese Hymn (Adeste Fideles) **11 11 11 11**

"K" in RIPPON's *Selection*, 1787

J. F. WADE's, *Cantus Diversi*, 1751

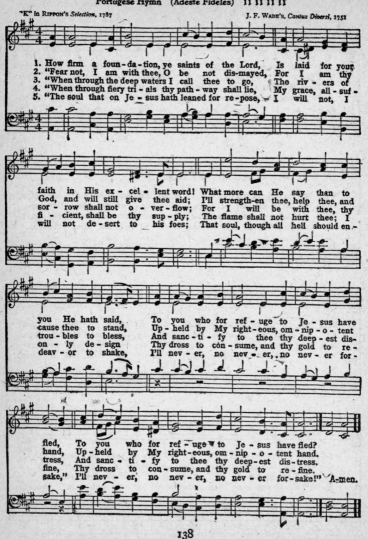

1. How firm a foun-da-tion, ye saints of the Lord, Is laid for your
2. "Fear not, I am with thee, O be not dis-mayed, For I am thy
3. "When through the deep waters I call thee to go, The riv-ers of
4. "When through fiery tri-als thy path-way shall lie, My grace, all-suf
5. "The soul that on Je-sus hath leaned for re-pose, I will not, I

faith in His ex-cel-lent word! What more can He say than to
God, and will still give thee aid; I'll strength-en thee, help thee, and
sor-row shall not o-ver-flow; For I will be with thee, thy
fi-cient, shall be thy sup-ply; The flame shall not hurt thee; I
will not de-sert to his foes; That soul, though all hell should en-

you He hath said, To you who for ref-uge to Je-sus have
cause thee to stand, Up-held by My right-eous, om-nip-o-tent
trou-bles to bless, And sanc-ti-fy to thee thy deep-est dis-
on-ly de-sign Thy dross to con-sume, and thy gold to re-
deav-or to shake, I'll nev-er, no nev-er, no nev-er for-

fled, To you who for ref-uge to Je-sus have fled?
hand, Up-held by My right-eous, om-nip-o-tent hand.
tress, And sanc-ti-fy to thee thy deep-est dis-tress.
fine, Thy dross to con-sume, and thy gold to re-fine.
sake," I'll nev-er, no nev-er, no nev-er for-sake!" A-men.

Now Thank We All Our God

Nun Danket 6 7 6 7 6 6 6 6

Martin Rinkart, 1636
Tr. Catherine Winkworth, 1858

Johann Cruger, 1647

1. Now thank we all our God
2. O may this boun-teous God
3. All praise and thanks to God,

With heart and hands and voic - es,
Through all our life be near us,
The Fa - ther, now be giv - en,

Who won-drous things hath done, In whom His world re - joic - es;
With ev - er joy - ful hearts And bless - ed peace to cheer us;
The Son, and Him who reigns With them in high - est heav - en,

Who, from our moth - ers' arms Hath blessed us on our way
And keep us in His grace, And guide us when per - plexed,
The one e - ter - nal God, Whom earth and heaven a - dore;

With count-less gifts of love, And still is ours to - day.
And free us from all ills In this world and the next.
For thus it was, is now, And shall be ev - er - more. A - men.

119

Abide with Me

Eventide 10 10 10 10

HENRY F. LYTE, 1847

WILLIAM H. MONK, 1861

1. A - bide with me; fast falls the e - ven tide;
2. Swift to its close ebbs out life's lit - tle day;
3. Not a brief glance I beg, a pass - ing word,
4. I need Thy pres - ence eve - ry pass - ing hour;
5. Hold Thou Thy cross be - fore my clos - ing eyes;

The dark - ness deep - ens, Lord, with me a - bide;
Earth's joys grow dim, its glo - ries pass a - way;
But as Thou dwell'st with Thy dis - ci - ples, Lord,-
What but Thy grace can foil the tempt - er's power?
Shine through the gloom, and point me to the skies;

When oth - er help - ers fail, and com - forts flee,
Change and de - cay in all a - round I see;
Fam - il - iar, con - de - scend - ing, pa - tient, free;
Who like Thy - self my guide and stay can be?
Heaven's morn - ing breaks, and earth's vain shad - ows flee;

Help of the help - less, O a - bide with me.
O Thou, who chang - est not, a - bide with me.
Come, not to so - journ, but a - bide, with me.
Through cloud and sun - shine, O a - bide with me.
I tri - umph still, if Thou a - bide with me. A-men.

Lead, Kindly Light

Lux Benigna   10 4 10 4 10 10

John H. Newman, 1833

John B. Dykes, 1865

1. Lead, kind-ly Light, a-mid th' en-cir-cling gloom, Lead Thou me on.
2. I was not ev - er thus, nor prayed that Thou Shouldst lead me on;
3. So long Thy power hath blest me, sure it still Will lead me on,

The night is dark, and I am far from home; Lead Thou me on.
I loved to choose and see my path, but now Lead Thou me on.
O'er moor and fen, o'er crag and tor-rent, till The night is gone.

Keep Thou my feet; I do not ask to see
I loved the gar - ish day, and, spite of fears,
And with the morn those an-gel fa - ces smile

The dis - tant scene, one step e - nough for me.
Pride ruled my will; re - mem - ber not past years.
Which I have loved long since, and lost a - while. A - men.

God Be With You Till We Meet Again

Deus Vobiscum 9 8 8 9 With Refrain

Jeremiah E. Rankin. 1882

William G. Tomer. 1882

1. God be with you till we meet a - gain, By His counsels guide, up-hold you,
2. God be with you till we meet a - gain, 'Neath His wings pro-tect-ing hide you,
3. God be with you till we meet a - gain, When life's perils thick con-found you,
4. God be with you till we meet a - gain, Keep love's banner floating o'er you,

With His sheep se-cure - ly fold you, God be with you till we meet a - gain.
Dai - ly man - na still pro-vide you, God be with you till we meet a - gain.
Put His arms un - fail-ing round you, God be with you till we meet a - gain.
Smite death's threatening wave before you, God be with you till we meet a - gain.

REFRAIN

Till we meet, till we meet, Till we meet at Je - sus' feet;

Till we meet, till we meet, till we meet, Till we meet,

Till we meet, till we meet, God be with you till we meet a-gain. A-men.

Till we meet, till we meet, till we meet,

O Beautiful for Spacious Skies

Materna C. M. D.

KATHARINE LEE BATES, 1893, 1910   SAMUEL A. WARD, 1882

1. O beau-ti-ful for spa-cious skies, For am-ber waves of grain,
2. O beau-ti-ful for pil-grim feet Whose stern, im-passioned stress
3. O beau-ti-ful for he-roes proved In lib-er-at-ing strife,
4. O beau-ti-ful for pa-triot dream That sees, be-yond the years,

For pur-ple moun-tain maj-es-ties A-bove the fruit-ed plain!
A thor-ough-fare for free-dom beat A-cross the wil-der-ness!
Who more than self their coun-try loved, And mer-cy more than life!
Thine al-a-bas-ter cit-ies gleam Un-dimmed by hu-man tears!

A-mer-i-ca, A-mer-i-ca, God shed His grace on thee,
A-mer-i-ca, A-mer-i-ca, God mend thine ev-e-ry flaw,
A-mer-i-ca, A-mer-i-ca, May God thy gold re-fine,
A-mer-i-ca, A-mer-i-ca, God shed His grace on thee,

And crown thy good with broth-er-hood From sea to shin-ing sea.
Con-firm thy soul in self-con-trol, Thy lib-er-ty in law.
Till all suc-cess be no-ble-ness, And ev-e-ry gain di-vine.
And crown thy good with broth-er-hood From sea to shin-ing sea. A-men.

Watchman, tell Us of the Night

Watchman 7777 D

John Bowring, 1825

Lowell Mason, 1830

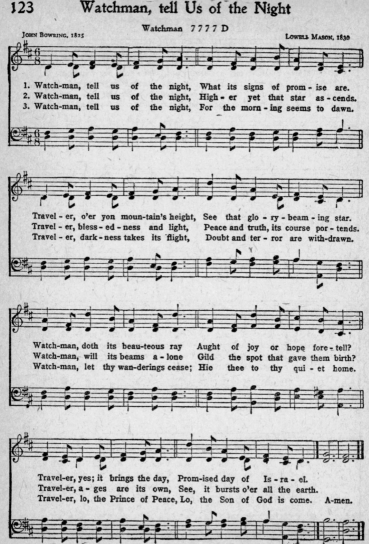

1. Watch-man, tell us of the night, What its signs of prom-ise are.
2. Watch-man, tell us of the night, High-er yet that star as-cends.
3. Watch-man, tell us of the night, For the morn-ing seems to dawn.

Travel-er, o'er yon moun-tain's height, See that glo-ry-beam-ing star.
Travel-er, bless-ed-ness and light, Peace and truth, its course por-tends.
Travel-er, dark-ness takes its flight, Doubt and ter-ror are with-drawn.

Watch-man, doth its beau-teous ray Aught of joy or hope fore-tell?
Watch-man, will its beams a-lone Gild the spot that gave them birth?
Watch-man, let thy wan-derings cease; Hie thee to thy qui-et home.

Travel-er, yes; it brings the day, Prom-ised day of Is-ra-el.
Travel-er, a-ges are its own, See, it bursts o'er all the earth.
Travel-er, lo, the Prince of Peace, Lo, the Son of God is come. A-men.

124 Blessed Assurance, Jesus is Mine

Blessed Assurance   9 10 9 9   With Refrain

FANNY J. CROSBY, 1820-1915   MRS. JOSEPH F. KNAPP, 1873

1. Bless-ed as-sur-ance, Je-sus is mine! O what a fore-taste of
2. Per-fect sub-mis-sion, per-fect de-light, Vis-ions of rap-ture now
3. Per-fect sub-mis-sion, all is at rest, I in my Sav-iour am

glo-ry di-vine! Heir of sal-va-tion, purchased of God, Born of his
burst on my sight. An-gels de-scend-ing, bring from a-bove Ech-oes of
hap-py and blest, Watching and wait-ing, looking a-bove, Filled with his

REFRAIN

Spir-it, washed in his blood.
mer-cy, whis-pers of love. This is my sto-ry, this is my song,
good-ness, lost in his love.

Prais-ing my Sav-iour all the day long; This is my sto-ry,

this is my song, Praising my Sav-iour all the day long. A-men.

125 All the Way My Saviour Leads Me

All the Way _ 8787D

FANNY J. CROSBY, 1820-1915

ROBERT LOWRY, 1875

1. All the way my Sav-iour leads me; What have I to ask be-side?
2. All the way my Sav-iour leads me; Cheers each wind-ing path I tread;
3. All the way my Sav-iour leads me; O the ful-ness of his love!

Can I doubt his ten-der mer-cy, Who thro' life has been my guide?
Gives me grace for ev-ery tri-al, Feeds me with the liv-ing bread;
Per-fect rest to me is prom-ised I my Fa-ther's house a-bove;

Heavenly peace, di-vin-est com-fort, Here by faith in him to swell;
Through my wea-ry steps may fal-ter, And my soul a-thirst may be,
When my spir-it clothed, im-mor-tal, Wings its flight to realms of day,

For I know what-e'er be-fall me, Je-sus so-eth all things well;
Gush-ing from the Rock be-fore me, Lo, a spring of joy I see;
This my song thro' end-less a-ges Je-sus led me all the way;

For I know what-e'er be-fall me, Je-sus do-eth all things well.
Gushing from the Rock be-fore me, Lo, a spring of joy I see.
This my song thro' end-less a-ges Je-sus led me all the way. A-men.

126 Throw Out the Life-Line

(May be sung as a Solo and Chorus)

Edwin S. Ufford

Edwin S. Ufford
Arranged by George C. Stebbins

1. Throw out the Life-Line a-cross the dark wave, There is a broth-er whom some one should save; Some-bod-y's broth-er! O who then, will dare To throw out the Life-Line, his per-il to share?

2. Throw out the Life-Line with hand quick and strong: Why do you tar-ry, why lin-ger so long? See! he is sink-ing; O has-ten to-day— And out with the Life-Boat! a-way, then, a-way!

3. Throw out the Life-Line to dan-ger-fraught men, Sink-ing in an-guish where you've nev-er been: Winds of temp-ta-tion and bil-lows of woe Will soon hurl them out where the dark wa-ters flow.

4. Soon will the sea-son of res-cue be o'er, Soon will they drift to e-ter-ni-ty's shore, Haste then, my broth-er, no time for de-lay, But throw out the Life-Line and save them to-day.

REFRAIN

Throw out the Life-Line! Throw out the Life-Line! Some one is drift-ing a-way; Throw out the Life-Line! Throw out the Life-Line! Some one is sinking to-day. A-men.

127 Nearer the Cross

Knapp Irregular

FANNY J. CROSBY

MRS. J. F. KNAPP

1. "Near-er the cross!" my heart can say, I am com-ing near-er; Near-er the
2. Near-er the Christian's mer-cy seat, I am com-ing near-er; Feasting my
3. Near-er in pray'r my hope as-pires I am com-ing near-er; Deep-er the

cross from day to day, I am com-ing near-er; Near-er the cross where
soul on man-na sweet I am com-ing near-er; Stronger in faith, more
love my soul de-sires, I am com-ing near-er; Near-er the end of

Je-sus died, Near-er the foun-tain's crim-son tide Near-er my Sav-iour's
clear I see Je-sus who gave Him-self for me; Near-er to Him I
toil and care, Near-er the joy I long to share, Near-er the crown I

wound-ed side, I am com-ing near-er, I am com-ing near-er.
still would be: Still I'm com-ing near-er, Still I'm com-ing near-er.
soon shall wear: I am com-ing near-er, I am com-ing near-er.

Eternal Father, Strong to Save

Melita 888888

WILLIAM WHITING, 1860

JOHN B. DYKES, 1861

1. E - ter - nal Fa - ther, strong to save, Whose arm doth bind the rest - less wave, Who bidd'st the might - y o - cean deep, Its own ap - point - ed lim - its keep; O hear us when we cry to Thee For those in per - il on the sea.

2. O Sav - iour, whose al - might - y word The winds and waves sub - mis - sive heard, Who walk - ed'st on the foam - ing deep, And calm a - midst its rage didst sleep; O hear us when we cry to Thee For those in per - il on the sea.

3. O Sa - cred Spir - it, who didst brood Up - on the cha - os dark and rude, Who bad'st its an - gry tu - mult cease, And gav - est light and life and peace; O hear us when we cry to Thee For those in per - il on the sea.

4. O Trin - i - ty of love and power, Our breth - ren shield in dan - ger's hour; From rock and tem - pest, fire and foe, Pro - tect them where - so - e'er they go, Thus ev - er let there rise to Thee Glad hymns of praise from land and sea. A - men.

129 There Were Ninety and Nine

The Ninety and Nine Irregular

Elizabeth C. Clephane

Ira D. Sankey

1. There were ninety and nine that safe-ly lay, In the shel-ter of the
2. "Lord, Thou hast here Thy nine-ty and nine; Are they not enough for
3. But none of the ransomed ev - er knew How deep were the wa - ters
4. "Lord, whence are those blood-drops all the way That mark out the mountain's
5. But all through the mountains, thun-der-riv'n, And up from the rock - y

fold, But one was out on the hills a - way, Far
Thee?" But the Shep - herd made answer: "This of mine Has
crossed; Nor how dark was the night that the Lord passed through Ere He
track?" "They were shed for one who had gone a - stray Ere the
steep, There a - rose a glad cry to the gate of heav'n, "Re -

rit.

off from the gates of gold— A - way on the moun - tains
wan - dered a - way from me, And al - tho' the road be
found His sheep that was lost. Out in the des - ert He
Shep-herd could bring him back." "Lord, whence are Thy hands so
joice! I have found my sheep!" And the an - gels ech-oed a -

wild and bare, A - way from the ten - der Shep - herd's care,
rough and steep, I go to the des - ert to find my sheep,
heard its cry— Sick and help-less, and read - y to die;
rent and torn?" "They're pierced to - night by many a thorn;
round the throne, "Re - joice, for the Lord brings back His own!

There Were Ninety and Nine

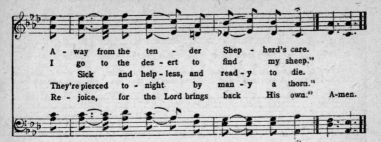

A - way from the ten - der Shep - herd's care.
I go to the des - ert to find my sheep."
Sick and help - less, and read - y to die.
They're pierced to - night by man - y a thorn."
Re - joice, for the Lord brings back His own." A-men.

130   O for a Thousand Tongues

Azmon C. M.

Charles Wesley

Carl G. Glaser
Arr. by Lowell Mason

1. O for a thou - sand tongues to sing   My great Re-deem-er's praise,
2. My gra - cious Mas - ter and my God,   As - sist me to pro - claim,
3. Je - sus! the name that charms our fears,   That bids our sor - rows cease;
4. He breaks the power of can-celed sin,   He sets the pris - oner free;
5. Hear Him, ye deaf; His praise, ye dumb,   Your loos-ened tongues em-ploy;

The glo - ries of my God and King, The tri - umphs of His grace.
To spread through all the earth a-broad, The hon-ors of Thy name.
'Tis mu-sic in the sin-ner's ears, 'Tis life, and health, and peace.
His blood can make the foul - est clean; His blood a-vailed for me.
Ye blind, be-hold your Sav-iour come; And leap, ye lame, for joy. A - men.

Who is on the Lord's Side

Armageddon 6 5 6 5 6 5 D

FRANCES R. HAVERGAL, 1877

ARR. by JOHN GOSS, 1871

1. Who is on the Lord's side? Who will serve the King? Who will be His
2. Not for weight of glo - ry, Not for crown and palm, En - ter we the
3. Je - sus, Thou hast bought us, Not with gold or gem, But with Thine own
4. Fierce may be the con - flict, Strong may be the foe, But the King's own

help - ers Oth - er lives to bring? Who will leave the world's side?
ar - my, Raise the war - rior psalm; But for love that claim - eth
life - blood, For Thy di - a - dem. With Thy bless - ing fill - ing
ar - my, None can o - ver - throw. Round His stand - ard rang - ing

Who will face the foe? Who is on the Lord's side? Who for
Lives for whom He died; He whom Je - sus nam - eth Must be
Each who comes to Thee, Thou hast made us will - ing, Thou hast
Vic - tory is se - cure; For His truth un - chang - ing Makes the

Him will go? By Thy call of mer - cy, By Thy grace di - vine,
on His side. By Thy love con - strain - ing, By Thy grace di - vine,
made us free. By Thy grand re - demp - tion, By Thy grace di - vine,
tri - umph sure. Joy - ful - ly en - list - ing By Thy grace di - vine,

We are on the Lord's side, Sav - iour, we are Thine. A - men.

132 Sing Them Over Again to Me

Wonderful Words of Life 868666 With Refrain

P. P. B.   P. P. BLISS

1. Sing them o - ver a - gain to me, Won - der - ful words of Life;
2. Christ, the bless - ed One, gives to all, Won - der - ful words of Life;
3. Sweet - ly ech - o the gos - pel call, Won - der - ful words of Life;

Let me more of their beau - ty see, Won - der - ful words of Life.
Sin - ner, list to the lov - ing call, Won - der - ful words of Life.
Of - fer par - don and peace to all, Won - der - ful words of Life.

Words of life and beau - ty, Teach me faith and du - ty:
All so free - ly giv - en, Woo - ing us to Heav - en:
Je - sus, on - ly Sav - iour, Sanc - ti - fy for - ev - er:

REFRAIN

Beau - ti - ful words, won - der - ful words, Won - der - ful words of Life.

Beau - ti - ful words, won - der - ful words, Won - der - ful words of Life.

My Hope Is Built

The Solid Rock   L. M.   With Refrain

Rev. Edward Mote

William B. Bradbury

1. My hope is built on noth-ing less Than Je-sus' blood and
2. When dark-ness veils His love-ly face, I rest on His un-
3. His oath, His cov-e-nant, His blood, Sup-port me in the
4. When He shall come with trum-pet sound, O, may I then in

right-eous-ness; I dare not trust the sweet-est frame, But
chang-ing grace; In ev-ery high and storm-y gale, My
whelm-ing flood; When all a-round my soul gives way, He
Him be found; Dress'd in His right-eous-ness a-lone, Fault-

Refrain

whol-ly lean on Je-sus' name.
anch-or holds with-in the vail. On Christ, the sol-id rock I stand;
then is all my hope and stay.
less to stand be-fore the throne!

All oth-er ground is sink-ing sand, All oth-er ground is sink-ing sand.

134 Marching with the Heroes

Rosmore 6 5 6 5 D With Refrain

WILLIAM C. TARRANT, 1853-1928   HENRY G. TREMBATH, 1844-1908

1. Marching with the he - roes, Com-rades of the strong, Lift we hearts and voic-es
2. Glo - ry to the he - roes, Who in days of old Trod the path of du - ty,
3. So we sing the sto - ry Of the brave and true, Till a-mong the he - roes

As we march a - long; O the joy-ful mu - sic All in cho-rus raise!
Faith-ful, wise, and bold, For the right un - flinch-ing, Strong the weak to save,
We are he - roes too; Loy-al to our Cap-tain Like the men of yore,

REFRAIN

Theirs the song of tri - umph, Ours the song of praise. Marching with the he - roes,
War - riors all and free-men Fight-ing for the slave. Glo - ry to the he - roes
March-ing with the he - roes On-ward ev - er-more. O the joy-ful mu - sic

Comrades of the strong, Lift we hearts and voic-es As we march a - long.
Who in days of old Trod the path of du - ty, Faith-ful, wise, and bold.
All in cho-rus raise! Theirs the song of tri-umph, Ours the song of praise. A-men.

135 On Jordan's Stormy Banks

Jordan's Banks C. M. With Refrain

Samuel Stennett

Arr. by R. M. McIntosh

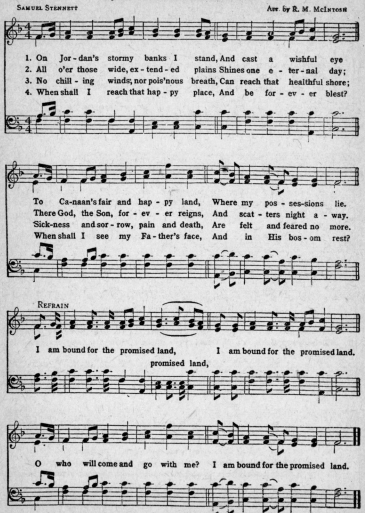

1. On Jor-dan's stormy banks I stand, And cast a wishful eye
2. All o'er those wide, ex-tend-ed plains Shines one e-ter-nal day;
3. No chill-ing winds; nor pois'nous breath, Can reach that healthful shore;
4. When shall I reach that hap-py place, And be for-ev-er blest?

To Ca-naan's fair and hap-py land, Where my pos-ses-sions lie.
There God, the Son, for-ev-er reigns, And scat-ters night a-way.
Sick-ness and sor-row, pain and death, Are felt and feared no more.
When shall I see my Fa-ther's face, And in His bos-om rest?

REFRAIN

I am bound for the promised land, I am bound for the promised land.
promised land,

O who will come and go with me? I am bound for the promised land.

Love Divine, all Loves Excelling

Beecher 8 7 8 7 D

CHARLES WESLEY, 1747

JOHN ZUNDEL, 1870

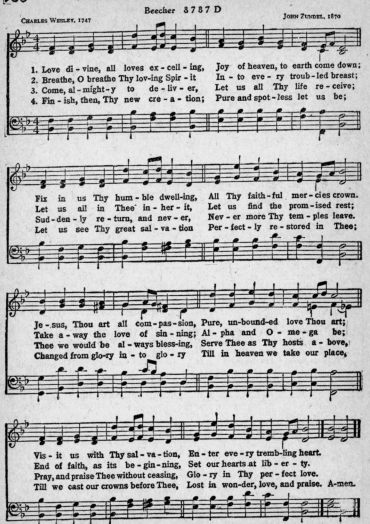

1. Love di-vine, all loves ex-cell-ing, Joy of heaven, to earth come down;
2. Breathe, O breathe Thy lov-ing Spir-it In-to eve-ry troub-led breast;
3. Come, al-might-y to de-liv-er, Let us all Thy life re-ceive;
4. Fin-ish, then, Thy new cre-a-tion; Pure and spot-less let us be;

Fix in us Thy hum-ble dwell-ing, All Thy faith-ful mer-cies crown.
Let us all in Thee in-her-it, Let us find the prom-ised rest;
Sud-den-ly re-turn, and nev-er, Nev-er more Thy tem-ples leave.
Let us see Thy great sal-va-tion Per-fect-ly re-stored in Thee;

Je-sus, Thou art all com-pas-sion, Pure, un-bound-ed love Thou art;
Take a-way the love of sin-ning; Al-pha and O-me-ga be;
Thee we would be al-ways bless-ing, Serve Thee as Thy hosts a-bove,
Changed from glo-ry in-to glo-ry Till in heaven we take our place,

Vis-it us with Thy sal-va-tion, En-ter eve-ry tremb-ling heart.
End of faith, as its be-gin-ning, Set our hearts at lib-er-ty.
Pray, and praise Thee without ceasing, Glo-ry in Thy per-fect love.
Till we cast our crowns before Thee, Lost in won-der, love, and praise. A-men.

137 Not Worthy Lord, to Gather

Morecambe 10 10 10 10

Edward H. Bickersteth, 1825-1906

Frederick C. Atkinson, 1841-1897

1. Not wor-thy, Lord, to gath-er up the crumbs
2. I am not wor-thy to be thought thy child,
3. I hear thy voice; thou bidd'st me come and rest;
4. My praise can on-ly breathe it-self in prayer,

With trem-bling hand, that from thy ta-ble fall,
Nor sit the last or low-est at thy board;
I come, I kneel, I clasp thy pierc-ed feet;
My prayer can on-ly lose it-self in thee;

A wea-ry, heav-y-la-den sin-ner comes
Too long a wan-derer, and too oft be-guiled,
Thou bidd'st me take my place, a wel-come guest,
Dwell thou for-ev-er in my heart, and there,

To plead thy prom-ise and o-bey thy call.
I on-ly ask one rec-on-cil-ing word.
A-mong thy saints, and of thy ban-quet eat.
Lord, let me sup with thee; sup thou with me. A-men.

138 Take the Name of Jesus with You

Precious Name 8 7 8 7 With Refrain

Mrs. Lydia Baxter, 1809-1879

William H. Doane, 1832-1913

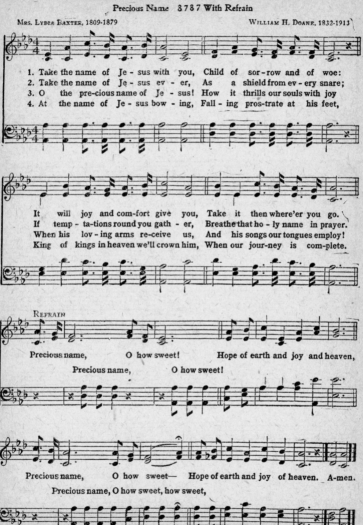

1. Take the name of Je - sus with you, Child of sor - row and of woe:
2. Take the name of Je - sus ev - er, As a shield from ev - ery snare;
3. O the pre-cious name of Je - sus! How it thrills our souls with joy
4. At the name of Je - sus bow - ing, Fall - ing pros-trate at his feet,

It will joy and com-fort give you, Take it then where'er you go.
If temp - ta-tions round you gath - er, Breathe that ho - ly name in prayer.
When his lov - ing arms re-ceive us, And his songs our tongues employ!
King of kings in heaven we'll crown him, When our jour-ney is com-plete.

REFRAIN

Precious name, O how sweet! Hope of earth and joy and heaven,

Precious name, O how sweet!

Precious name, O how sweet— Hope of earth and joy of heaven. A-men.

Precious name, O how sweet, how sweet,

139 Mine Eyes Have Seen the Glory

Battle Hymn of the Republic 15 15 15 6 With Refrain

JULIA WARD HOWE, 1861   WILLIAM STEFFE, 1852

1. Mine eyes have seen the glo - ry of the
2. I have seen Him in the watch - fires of a
3. He has sound - ed forth His trum - pet that shall
4. In the beau - ty of the lil - ies Christ was

com - ing of the Lord; He is tramp-ling out the vin - tage where the
hun - dred cir - cling camps; They have build-ed Him an al - tar in the
nev - er call re - treat; He is sift - ing out the hearts of men be-
born a - cross the sea, With a glo - ry in His bos - om that trans-

grapes of wrath are stored; He hath loosed the fate - ful light - ning of His
eve - ning dews and damps; I have read His right-eous sen-tence by the
fore His judg-ment-seat; O be swift, my soul, to an - swer Him, be-
fig - ures you and me; As He died to make men ho - ly let us

ter - ri - ble swift sword; His truth is march - ing on.
dim and flar - ing lamps; His day is march - ing on.
ju - bi - lant, my feet; Our God is march - ing on.
die to make men free, While God is march - ing on.

Mine Eyes Have Seen the Glory

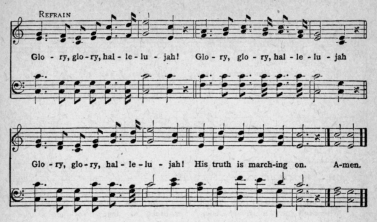

REFRAIN

Glo - ry, glo - ry, hal - le - lu - jah! Glo - ry, glo - ry, hal - le - lu - jah

Glo - ry, glo - ry, hal - le - lu - jah! His truth is march-ing on. A - men.

140 A Charge to Keep I Have

Boylston S. M.

CHARLES WESLEY

LOWELL MASON

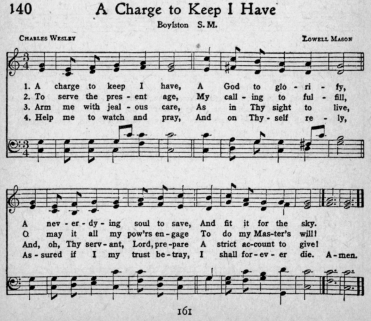

1. A charge to keep I have, A God to glo - ri - fy,
2. To serve the pres - ent age, My call - ing to ful - fill,
3. Arm me with jeal - ous care, As in Thy sight to live,
4. Help me to watch and pray, And on Thy - self re - ly,

A nev - er - dy - ing soul to save, And fit it for the sky.
O, may it all my pow'rs en - gage To do my Mas-ter's will!
And, oh, Thy serv - ant, Lord, pre - pare A strict ac-count to give!
As - sured if I my trust be - tray, I shall for - ev - er die. A - men.

The National Anthem

The Star-Spangled Banner Irregular

FRANCIS S. KEY, 1814

JOHN S. SMITH, 1775

1. O   say, can you   see,   by the dawn's ear - ly light,
2. On the shore dim - ly   seen   through the mists of   the   deep,
3. O   thus be it   ev - er   when   free - men shall stand

What so proud - ly we hailed   at the twi - light's last gleam - ing,
Where the foe's haught - y host   in dread si - lence re - pos - es,
Be - tween their loved homes and the war's des - o - la - tion;

Whose broad stripes and bright stars, through the per - il - ous · fight,
What is   that which the breeze, o'er   the tow - er - ing steep
Blest with vic - tory and peace, may   the Heaven-res - cued land

O'er the ram - parts we watched were so gal - lant - ly stream - ing?
As it fit - ful - ly blows, half con - ceals, half dis - clos - es?
Praise the Power that hath. made   and pre - served us a   na - tion.

The National Anthem

And the rock - ets' red glare, the bombs burst - ing in air,
Now it catch - es the gleam of the morn - ing's first beam,
Then con - quer we must, when our cause it is just,

Gave proof through the night that our flag was still there;
In full glo - ry re - flect - ed now shines on the stream;
And this be our mot - to, "In God is our trust;"

O say, does the Star - span - gled Ban - ner yet wave
'Tis the Star - span - gled Ban - ner— O long may it wave
And the Star - span - gled Ban - ner in tri - umph shall wave

O'er the land of the free and the home of the brave?
O'er the land of the free and the home of the brave.
O'er the land of the free and the home of the brave.

142 God of the Nations, Who from Dawn

Summerford 10 10 10 10

W. RUSSELL BOWIE, 1913

JOHN T. GRIMLEY, 1887

1. God of the Na - tions, who from dawn of days
2. Thine an - cient might did break the Phar - aoh's boast,
3. Thy hand has led a - cross the hun - gry sea
4. Then, for Thy grace to grow in broth - er - hood

Hast led Thy peo - ple in their widen - ing ways,
Thou wast the shield for Is - rael's march - ing host,
The ea - ger peo - ples flock - ing to be free,
For hearts a - flame to serve Thy des - tined good,

Through whose deep pur - pose stran - ger thou - sands stand
And, all the a - ges through, past crumb - ling throne
And from the breeds of earth, Thy si - lent sway
For faith, and will to win what faith shall see,

Here in the bor - ders of your prom - ised land.
And bro - ken fet - ter, Thou hast brought Thine own.
Fash - ions the na - tion of the broaden - ing day.
God of Thy peo - ple, hear us cry to Thee. A - men.

Words copyright, 1914, by Survey Associates. Copyright assigned to A. S. Barnes and Co., Inc., 1941. Copyright renewed, 1942.

God Bless America

(Introduced by Kate Smith, Armistice Day, 1938)

F major – Count 2

Words and Music by
IRVING BERLIN

143

March time

God bless A-mer-i-ca, Land that I love, Stand be-

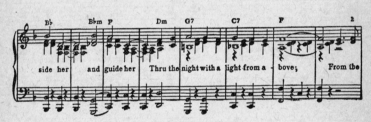

side her and guide her Thru the night with a light from a-bove; From the

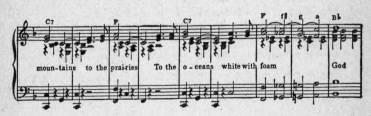

moun-tains to the prai-ries To the o-ceans white with foam God

bless A-mer-i-ca, My home sweet home. home.

Copyright 1939 by Irving Berlin, Inc. Used by permission.

My Country, 'tis of Thee

America 6646664

SAMUEL F. SMITH, 1832

HENRY CAREY, 1740

1. My coun-try, 'tis of thee, Sweet land of lib-er-ty,
2. My na-tive coun-try, thee, Land of the no-ble free,
3. Let mu-sic swell the breeze, And ring from all the trees
4. Our fa-ther's God, to thee, Au-thor of lib-er-ty,

Of thee I sing; Land where my fa-thers died, Land of the
Thy name I love; I love thy rocks and rills, Thy woods and
Sweet free-dom's song; Let mor-tal tongues a-wake; Let all that
To thee we sing; Long may our land be bright With free-dom's

pil-grim's pride, From ev-er-y moun-tain side Let free-dom ring!
tem-pled hills; My heart with rap-ture thrills, Like that a-bove.
breathe partake; Let rocks their si-lence break, The sound pro-long.
ho-ly light; Pro-tect us by thy might, Great God, our King. A-men.

145

God Bless Our Native Land

Dort 6646664

SIEGFRIED A. MAHLMANN, 1815
Tr by C. T. BROOKS, 1833, and J. S. DWIGHT, 1844

LOWELL MASON, 1832

1. God bless our na-tive land, Firm may she ev-er stand Through storm and
2. For her our prayers shall rise To God a-bove the skies, On him we

God Bless Our Native Land

night; When the wild tem-pests rave, Rul-er of wind and wave,
wait; Thou who art ev-er nigh, Guarding with watch-ful eye,

Do thou our coun-try save By thy great might.
To thee a-loud we cry, God save the state. A-men.

146 Sleep, Comrades Sleep!
Hymn for Memorial Day 7 8 12 8

HENRY WADSWORTH LONGFELLOW   WILLIAM M. FELTON

1. Sleep, com-rades, sleep, sleep and rest! On this
2. Rest, com-rades, rest, rest and sleep! The thoughts of
3. Your si-lent tents, tents of green, We deck with

field of the ground-ed arms Where foes no more mo-lest, Nor
men shall ev-er be As sen-ti-nels, to keep Your
flow'rs, with fra-grant flow'rs; Yours has the suf-f'ring been The

sen-try's shot a-larms! Sleep, com-rades, sleep! Sleep, com-rades, sleep!
rest from dan-ger free, Sleep, com-rades, sleep! Sleep, com-rades, sleep!
mem-'ry shall be ours, Sleep, com-rades, sleep! Sleep, com-rades, sleep!

147 Holy Spirit, Faithful Guide

Holy Spirit, Faithful Guide 7 7 7 7 D

MARCUS M. WELLS, 1815-1895

M. M. WELLS, 1815-1895

1. Ho - ly Spir - it, faith - ful Guide, Ev - er near the Christian's side,
2. Ev - er pres - ent, tru - est Friend, Ev - er near Thine aid to lend,
3. When our days of toil shall cease, Wait-ing still for sweet re - lease,

Gent - ly lead us by the hand, Pil - grims in a des - ert land.
Leave us not to doubt and fear, Grop - ing on in dark - ness drear;
Noth - ing left but heaven and prayer, Won - dering if our names are there;

Wea - ry souls for - e'er re - joice, While they hear that sweet - est voice,
When the storms are rag - ing sore, Hearts grow faint and hopes give o'er,
Wad - ing deep the dis - mal flood, Plead - ing naught but Je - sus' blood,

Whisp'ring soft - ly "Wan-d'rer, Come! Fol - low me, I'll guide thee home."
Whis - per soft - ly, "Wan-d'rer, come! Fol - low me, I'll guide thee home."
Whis - per soft - ly, "Wan-d'rer, come! Fol - low me, I'll guide thee home."

Nobody Knows the Trouble I've Seen

Spiritual

REFRAIN

No-bod-y knows the trou-ble I've seen, No-bod-y knows my sor-row;

No bod-y knows the trou-ble I've seen, Glo-ry hal-le-lu-jah!

FINE

DUET *somewhat faster* CHORUS

1. Some-times I'm up, some-times I'm down, Oh, yes, Lord!
2. Al-tho' you see me going 'long so, Oh, yes, Lord!
3. What makes old Sa-tan hate me so, Oh, yes, Lord!

DUET *D C. al Fine*

Some-times I'm al-most to the groun', Oh, yes, Lord!
I have my trou-bles here be-low, Oh, yes, Lord!
'Cause he got me once and let me go. Oh, yes, Lord!

Swing Low, Sweet Chariot

Spiritual

Swing low, sweet char - i - ot, Com-in' - a for to car - ry me home

Swing low, sweet char - i - ot, Com-in' - a for to car - ry me home.

1. I looked o - ver Jor - dan, and what did I see,
2. If you get there be - fore I do,
3. The bright - est day that ev - er I saw,
4. I'm some - times up and some - times down,

Com-in' - a for to car - ry me home? A band of an - gels a -
Com-in' - a for to car - ry me home; Tell all my friends I'm a -
Com-in' - a for to car - ry me home; When Je - sus washed my
Com-in' - a for to car - ry me home; But still my soul feels

com-in' aft - er me, Com-in' - a for to car - ry me home.
com - in' too, Com-in' - a for to car - ry me home.
sins a - way, Com-in' - a for to car - ry me home.
heav-en - ly bound, Com-in' - a for to car - ry me home.

Swing Low, Sweet Chariot

Swing low, sweet char - i - ot, Com-in' - a for to car-ry me home,

Swing low, sweet char - i - ot, Com-in' - a for to car-ry me home.

150 When Israel was in Egypt's Land

Spiritual

1. When Is - rael was in E - gypt's land: Let my peo-ple go, Op -
2. Thus saith the Lord bold Mo - ses said, Let my peo-ple go, If
3. No more shall they in bond-age toil, Let my peo-ple go, Let
4. O let us all from bond-age flee, Let my peo-ple go, And

pressed so hard they could not stand, Let my peo-ple go. Go down, Mo - ses,
not I'll smite your first-born dead, Let my peo-ple go. Go down, Mo - ses,
them come out with E-gypt's spoil, Let my peo-ple go. Go down, Mo - ses,
let us all in Christ be free, Let my peo-ple go. Go down, Mo - ses,

'Way down in E-gypt's land, Tell ole Pha-raoh, Let my peo-ple go.

Lord, I Want to be a Christian

Spiritual

1. Lord, I want to be a Chris-tian In-a my heart, in-a my
2. Lord, I want to be more lov-ing In-a my heart, in-a my
3. Lord, I want to be more ho-ly In-a my heart, in-a my
4. I don't want to be like Ju-das In-a my heart, in-a my
5. Lord, I want to be like Je-sus In-a my heart, in-a my

heart, Lord, I want to be a Chris-tian In-a my heart.
heart, Lord, I want to be more lov-ing In-a my heart.
heart, Lord, I want to be more ho-ly In-a my heart.
heart, I don't want to be like Ju-das In-a my heart.
heart, Lord, I want to be like Je-sus In-a my heart.

REFRAIN

In-a my heart, In-a my heart,
In-a my heart, In-a my heart,

Lord, I want to be a Chris-tian In-a my heart.
Lord, I want to be more lov-ing In-a my heart.
Lord, I want to be more ho-ly In-a my heart.
I don't want to be like Ju-das In-a my heart.
Lord, I want to be like Je-sus In-a my heart.

Steal Away

Spiritual

Steal a-way, steal a-way, steal a-way to Je-sus!

Steal a-way, steal a-way home, I ain't got long to stay here.

1. My Lord calls me, He calls me by the thun-der; The
2. Green trees are bend-ing, Poor sin-ners stand a trem-bling; The
3. My Lord calls me, He calls me by the light-ning; The

trum-pet sounds with-in a my soul: I ain't got long to stay here.

Were You There?

Spiritual

1. Were you there when they cru - ci - fied my Lord? (were you there?)
2. Were you there when they nailed Him to the tree? (to the tree?)
3. Were you there when they pierced Him in the side? (in the side?)
4. Were you there when the sun re - fused to shine? (were you there?)
5. Were you there when they laid Him in the tomb? (in the tomb?)

Were you there when they cru - ci - fied my Lord?
Were you there when they nailed Him to the tree?
Were you there when they pierced Him in the side?
Were you there when the sun re - fused to shine?
Were you there when they laid Him in the tomb?

Oh! Sometimes it caus - es me to trem - ble, trem - ble,
Oh! Sometimes it caus - es me to trem - ble, trem - ble,
Oh! Sometimes it caus - es me to trem - ble, trem - ble,
Oh! Sometimes it caus - es me to trem - ble, trem - ble,
Oh! Sometimes it caus - es me to trem - ble, trem - ble,

FINE

trem - ble, Were you there when they cru - ci - fied my Lord?
trem - ble, Were you there when they nailed Him to the tree?
trem - ble, Were you there when they pierced Him in the side?
trem - ble, Were you there when the sun re - fused to shine?
trem - ble, Were you there when they laid Him in the tomb?

There's a Church in the Valley

Little Brown Church

WILLIAM S. PITTS   WILLIAM S. PITTS

MALE VOICES, MELODY IN 2D TENOR

1. There's a church in the val-ley by the wild-wood, No love-li-er
2. How sweet on a clear, Sab-bath morn-ing, To list to the
3. There, close by the church in the val-ley, Lies one that I
4. There, close by the side of that loved one, 'Neath the tree where the

place in the dale; No spot is so dear to my child-hood As the
clear ring-ing bell; Its tones so sweet-ly are call-ing, O
loved so well; She sleeps, sweet-ly sleeps 'neath the wil-lows; Dis-
wild flow-ers bloom, When the fare-well hymn shall be chant-ed, I shall

D.S.—spot is so dear to my child-hood As the

REFRAIN   *Fine*

lit-tle brown church in the vale.   Come to the
come to the church in the vale.
turb not her rest in the vale.
rest by her side in the tomb.   O come, come, come, come, come, come,

lit-tle brown church in the vale.

D.S.

church in the wild - wood, O come to the church in the dale;   No
come, come, come, come, come, come, come, come. come, come, come, come, come.

'Mid Pleasures and Palaces

Home, Sweet Home

J. H. PAYNE

H. R. BISHOP

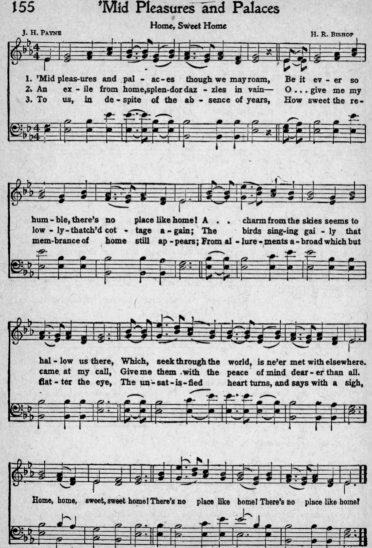

1. 'Mid pleas-ures and pal - ac - es though we may roam, Be it ev - er so
2. An ex - ile from home, splen-dor daz - zles in vain— O . . . give me my
3. To us, in de - spite of the ab - sence of years, How sweet the re-

hum - ble, there's no place like home! A . . charm from the skies seems to
low - ly - thatch'd cot - tage a - gain; The birds sing-ing gai - ly that
mem-brance of home still ap - pears; From al - lure - ments a - broad which but

hal - low us there, Which, seek through the world, is ne'er met with elsewhere.
came at my call, Give me them with the peace of mind dear - er than all.
flat - ter the eye, The un - sat - is - fied heart turns, and says with a sigh,

Home, home, sweet, sweet home! There's no place like home! There's no place like home!

156 Gone Are the Days

Old Black Joe

S. C. F.

Stephen C. Foster

1. Gone are the days when my heart was young and gay; Gone are my
2. Why do I weep when my heart should feel no pain? Why do I
3. Where are the hearts once so hap-py and so free? The chil-dren so

friends from the cot-ton fields a-way; Gone from the earth to a
sigh that my friends come not a-gain? Griev-ing for forms now de-
dear that I held up-on my knee? Gone to the shore where my

bet-ter land I know, . I hear their gen-tle voic-es call-ing, "Old Black Joe!"
part-ed long a-go, I hear their gen-tle voic-es call-ing, "Old Black Joe!"
soul has long'd to go, I hear their gen-tle voic-es call-ing, "Old Black Joe!"

CHORUS

D.S. al Fine.

I'm com-ing, I'm com-ing, For my head is bend-ing low;

The Sun Shines Bright

My Old Kentucky Home

Stephen C. Foster

1. The sun shines bright in the old Ken-tuck-y home, 'Tis sum-mer, the dark-ies are gay; The corn-top's ripe and the mead-ow's in the bloom, While the birds make mu-sic all the day. The young folks roll on the lit-tle cab-in floor, All mer-ry all hap-py and bright; By'n - by hard times comes a - knock-ing at the door, Then my old Ken-tuck-y home, good-night!

2. They hunt no more for the pos-sum and the coon, On the mead-ow, the hill and the shore; They sing no more by the glim-mer of the moon, On the bench by the old cab-in door. The day goes by like a shad-ow o'er the heart, With sor-row where all was de-light; The time has come when the dark-ies have to part, Then my old Ken-tuck-y home, good-night!

3. The head must bow and the back will have to bend, Wher - ev - er the dark-ey may go; A few more days, and the trou-ble all will end, In the field where the su-gar canes grow; A few more days for to tote the wea-ry load,— No mat-ter 'twill nev-er be light; A few more days till we tot - ter on the road, Then my old Ken-tuck-y home, good-night!

The Sun Shines Bright

REFRAIN

Weep no more, my la-dy, O weep no more to-day! We will sing one song for the old Ken-tuck-y home, For the old Ken-tuck-y home, far a-way.

158   How Can I Leave Thee

FRIEDRICH KÜCKEN

1. How can I leave thee! How can I from thee part! Thou on-ly
2. Blue is a flow'r-et Called the For-get-me-not, Wear it up-
3. Would I a bird were! Soon at thy side to be, Fal-con nor

hast my heart, Dear one, be-lieve. Thou hast this soul of mine
on thy heart, And think of me! Flow'r-et and hope may die,
hawk would fear, Speed-ing to thee. When, by the fow-ler slain,

So close-ly bound to thine, No oth-er can I love Save thee a-lone!
Yet love with us shall stay, That can-not pass a-way, Dear one, be-lieve.
I at thy feet should lie, Thou sad-ly shouldst com-plain, Joy-ful I'd die.

179

Sweet and Low

ALFRED TENNYSON

J. BARNBY

Larghetto

1. Sweet and low, sweet and low, Wind of the west - ern sea;
2. Sleep and rest, sleep and rest, Fa - ther will come to thee soon;

Low, low, breathe and blow, Wind of the west - ern sea;
Rest, rest, on moth - er's breast, Fa - ther will come to thee soon;

1. { O - ver the roll - ing wa - ters go, Come from the
   { O - - - ver the wa - ters go, Come
2. { Fa - ther will come to his babe in the nest, Sil - ver
   { Fa - - - ther will come to his babe, Sil - ver

{ dy - ing moon and blow, Blow him a - gain to me,
{ from the moon and blow, Blow him a - gain to me,
{ sails all out of the west, Un - der the sil - ver moon,
{ sails out of the west, Un - der the sil - ver moon,

Sweet and Low

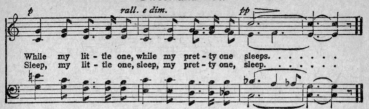

rall. e dim. *pp*

While my lit - tle one, while my pret - ty one sleeps. . . . . .
Sleep, my lit - tle one, sleep, my pret - ty one, sleep. . . . . .

160. Should Auld Acquaintance be Forgot

Auld Lang Syne

ROBERT BURNS

SCOTCH AIR

1. Should auld ac - quain - tance be for - got, And nev - er bro't to mind?
2. And here's a hand, my trust - y frien', And gie's a hand o' thine;

Should auld ac - quain - tance be for - got, And days of auld lang syne?
We'll tak' a cup o' kind - ness yet, For auld lang syne.

REFRAIN

For auld lang syne, my dear, For auld lang

syne; We'll tak' a cup o' kind - ness yet For auld lang syne.

161 Round de Meadows Am a-Ringing

Massa's In The Cold Ground

S. C. F.

STEPHEN C. FOSTER

1. Round de mead-ows am a - ring - ing   De dark - ies' mourn - ful song
2. When de au - tumn leaves were fall - ing,   When de days were cold,
3. Mas - sa makes de dark - ies love him,   Cayse he was so kind,

While de mock-ing bird am sing - ing,   Hap - py as de day am long.
'Twas hard to hear old Mas - sa call - ing,   Cayse he was so weak and old.
Now dey sad - ly weep a - bove him,   Mourn - ing cayse he leave dem be-hind.

Where de i - vy am a - creep - ing,   O'er de gras - sy mound,
Now de o - range trees am bloom - ing,   On de san - dy shore,
I can - not work be - fore to - mor - row,   Cayse de tear drop now;

Dere old Mas - sa am a - sleep - ing,   Sleep - ing in de cold, cold ground.
Now de sum - mer days am com - ing,   Mas - sa neb - ber calls no more.
I try to drive a - way my sor - row,   Pick - ing on de old ban - jo.

REFRAIN

Down   in   de   corn - field   Hear   dat mourn - ful   sound;

All de dark-ies am a-weep-ing, Mas-sa's in de cold, cold ground.

162   Way Down Upon the Swanee River

Old Folks At Home

STEPHEN C. FOSTER

S. C. F.

1. { Way down up-on de Swa-nee Riv-er, Far, far a-way,
     All up and down de whole cre-a-tion, Sad-ly I roam,
2. { All roun' de lit-tle farm I wan-der'd, When I was young;
     When I was play-ing with my broth-er, Hap-py was I;
3. { One lit-tle hut a-mong the bush-es, One that I love,
     When will I see de bees a-hum-ming All roun' de comb?

Dere's wha my heart is turn-ing ev-er, Dere's wha de old folks stay.
Still long-ing for de old plan-ta-tion, And for de old folks at home.
Den man-y hap-py days I squan-der'd, Man-y de songs I sung.
Oh! take me to my kind old moth-er, There let me live and die.
Still sad-ly to my mem-'ry rush-es, No mat-ter where I rove.
When will I hear de ban-jo tum-ming, Down in my good old home?

D.S. Oh! dark-ies how my heart grows wea-ry, Far from the old folks at home.

D.S.

All de world am sad and drear-y, Ev-'ry-where I roam;

183

163   Good Night Ladies

1. Good - night, la - dies!   Good - night, la - dies!   Good - night, la - dies!
2. Fare - well, la - dies!   Fare - well, la - dies!   Fare - well, la - dies!
3. Sweet dreams, la - dies!   Sweet dreams, la - dies!   Sweet dreams, la - dies!

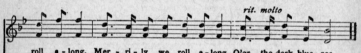

We're going to leave you now.   Mer - ri - ly we roll a - long, roll a - long,

roll a - long, Mer - ri - ly we roll a - long, O'er the dark blue sea.

164   Day is Done

Taps 3 3 3 3

1. Day is done, gone the sun, From the lake, from the hills, from the
2. Fad - ing light dims the sight, And a star gems the sky, gleam - ing
3. Then good night, peace - ful night, Till the light of the dawn shin - eth

sky;   All is well, safe - ly rest;   God is nigh.
bright.   From a - far draw - ing nigh,   Falls the night.
bright;   God is near, do not fear,   Friend, good - night.

184

Index of First Lines

(C) Creed; (CH) Catholic Hymn; (FS) Folk Song; (H) Hymn; (O-) Orchestration A and N Hymnal; (P) Prayer; (RR) Responsive Reading

185

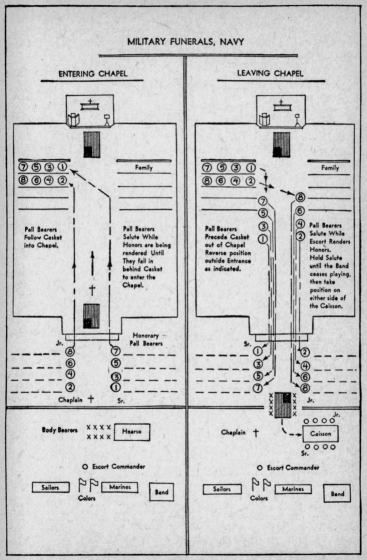

MILITARY FUNERALS, NAVY

ENTERING CHAPEL

Family

Pall Bearers Follow Casket into Chapel.

Pall Bearers Salute While Honors are being rendered Until They fall in behind Casket to enter the Chapel.

Jr.

Honorary — Pall Bearers

Chaplain Sr.

Body Bearers X X X X   Hearse
X X X X

O Escort Commander

Sailors   Marines   Band
Colors

LEAVING CHAPEL

Family

Pall Bearers Precede Casket out of Chapel Reverse position outside Entrance as indicated.

Pall Bearers Salute While Escort Renders Honors. Hold Salute until the Band ceases playing, then take position on either side of the Caisson.

Sr.

Jr.

Chaplain   Caisson

O Escort Commander

Sailors   Marines   Band
Colors

MILITARY FUNERALS, NAVY

THE PROCESSION

o Escort Commander

☐ Band

☐ Marines

⚑ Colors

☐ Blue Jackets

✝ Chaplain

⚑ Personal Flag if Deceased of Flag Rank.

Jr. o⊠o Caisson and Pall Bearers
x x
Sr. x x Body Bearers
x x

☐ Family

☐ Enlisted Men From Command of Deceased

☐ Officers From Command of Deceased

☐ Delegations

☐ Societies

If Honorary Pall Bearers ride they occupy car immediately in rear of caisson and the Body Bearers walk on either side of the Caisson.

AT THE GRAVE

| Band | | Marines | Colors | Sailors |

o

Bugler ☐ oooooooooo

Chaplain and Cemetery Rep. ✝ ⊠

Body Bearers and Casket x x x x

Honorary Pall Bearers o o o

Family ↑

Pall Bearers Salute while casket is being removed from caisson and until it has passed between them—

Jr. o ✝ ⊠ o
Pall Bearers o o
o o Sr.

Salute at Grave during Volleys and Taps.

Curb

Caisson | x x x x
x x x x

Family Cars

RECEPTION OF REMAINS AT ENTRANCE TO CEMETERY

☐ Band

☐ Marines

⚑ Colors

☐ Blue Jackets

Escort Commander o

Hearse ☐   Caisson ☐

Body Bearers x x x x x x

o
o
o
o
o
o
Honorary Pall Bearers

Chaplain ✝

☐ Family Cars

Pall Bearers Salute while Honors are being rendered hold Salute until Band ceases Playing.

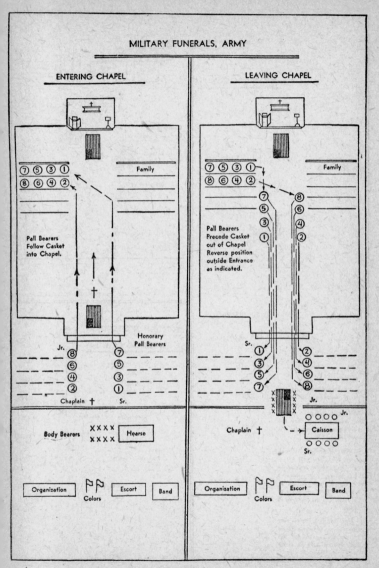

MILITARY FUNERALS, ARMY

ENTERING CHAPEL

Family

⑦ ⑤ ③ ①
⑧ ⑥ ④ ②

Pall Bearers
Follow Casket
into Chapel.

Honorary
Pall Bearers

Jr.

⑧   ⑦
⑥   ⑤
④   ③
②   ①

Chaplain †   Sr.

Body Bearers   XXXX
    XXXX   Hearse

Organization   Colors   Escort   Band

LEAVING CHAPEL

Family

⑦ ⑤ ③ ①
⑧ ⑥ ④ ②

⑦   ⑧
⑤   ⑥
③   ④
①   ②

Pall Bearers
Precede Casket
out of Chapel.
Reverse position
outside Entrance
as indicated.

Sr.

①   ②
③   ④
⑤   ⑥
⑦   ⑧

Jr.

Chaplain †   Caisson

Sr.

Organization   Colors   Escort   Band

MILITARY FUNERALS, ARMY

AT THE GRAVE

Band | Escort | Colors | Organization

Bugler

Chaplain and Cemetery Rep.

Body Bearers and Casket

Honorary Pall Bearers

Family

THE PROCESSION

Band

Escort

Colors

Chaplain

Jr. Caisson and Pall Bearers

Sr. Body Bearers

Family

Officers

Enlisted men

Societies

Jr. Pall Bearers Sr.

Curb

Caisson

Family Cars

RECEPTION OF REMAINS AT ENTRANCE TO CEMETERY

Band

Escort

Escort Commander

Colors

Organization

Hearse | Caisson

Body Bearers

Honorary Pall Bearers

Chaplain

Family Cars

NOTE:

While honors are being rendered honorary pall bearers hold the headdress over the left breast, except in inclement weather when they remain covered and execute the hand salute:

(1) At entrance of a chapel, (2) At chapel exit, (3) At reception of remains at entrance to cemetery, (4) At removing of remains from caisson or hearse and (5) during firing of the salute and the sounding of Taps.

If Honorary Pall Bearers ride they occupy car immediately in rear of caisson and the Body Bearers walk on either side of the Caisson.

The Prayer of a Midshipman

Almighty Father, whose way is in the sea and whose paths are in the great waters, whose command is over all and whose love never faileth: Let me be aware of Thy presence and obedient to Thy will. Keep me true to my best self, guarding me against dishonesty in purpose and in deed, and helping me so to live that I can stand unashamed and unafraid before my shipmates, my loved ones, and Thee. Protect those in whose love I live. Give me the will to do the work of a man and to accept my share of responsibilities with a strong heart and a cheerful mind. Make me considerate of those intrusted to my leadership and faithful to the duties my country has intrusted to me. Let my uniform remind me daily of the traditions of the Service of which I am a part. If I am inclined to doubt, steady my faith; if I am tempted, make me strong to resist; if I should miss the mark, give me courage to try again. Guide me with the light of truth and keep before me the life of Him by whose example and help I trust to obtain the answer to my prayer, Jesus Christ our Lord. Amen.

Cadet Prayer

O God, our Father, Thou Searcher of men's hearts, help us to draw near to Thee in sincerity and truth. May our religion be filled with gladness and may our worship of Thee be natural.

Strengthen and increase our admiration for honest dealing and clean thinking, and suffer not our hatred of hypocrisy and pretence ever to diminish. Encourage us in our endeavor to live above the common level of life. Make us to choose the harder right instead of the easier wrong, and never to be content with a half truth when the whole can be won. Endow us with courage that is born of loyalty to all that is noble and worthy, that scorns to compromise with vice and injustice and knows no fear when truth and right are in jeopardy. Guard us against flippancy and irreverence in the sacred things of life. Grant us new ties of friendship and new opportunities of service. Kindle our hearts in fellowship with those of a cheerful countenance, and soften our hearts with sympathy for those who sorrow and suffer. May we find genuine pleasure in clean and wholesome mirth and feel inherent disgust for all coarse-minded humour. Help us, in our work and in our play, to keep ourselves physically strong, mentally awake and morally straight, that we may the better maintain the honor of the Corps untarnished and unsullied, and acquit ourselves like men in our effort to realize the ideals of West Point in doing our duty to Thee and to our Country. All of which we ask in the name of the Great Friend and Master of men. Amen.